The Family Bed

The Family Bed

Tine Thevenin

AVERY PUBLISHING GROUP INC.
Wayne, New Jersey

DENNIS THE MENACE® used by permission of Hank Ketcham and © by News America Syndicate.

Cover design by Martin Hochberg and Rudy Shur

In-house Editor Jacqueline Balla
Layout designed by Diana Puglisi
Typeset by ACS Graphic Services, Fresh Meadows, NY

Library of Congress Cataloging-in Publication Data
Thevenin, Tine.
   The family bed.

   Bibliography: p.
   Includes index.
   1. Child rearing.　2. Child psychology.　3. Sleeping customs.　I. Title.
[HQ769.T466　1987]　　649'.1　　86-28739
ISBN 0-89529-357-9 (pbk.)

Printed in the United States of America

10　9　8　7　6　**5**　4　3　2　1

Contents

Dedicated to Yvonne and Michelle, with whom I have
shared so very much.

Acknowledgements

I wish to acknowledge the following persons with my deeply-felt gratitude:

Helen Wessel, for first suggesting that I turn my original, ninety-page research report into a book, and for being the first one to make me feel elated when she said, "I could hardly put the manuscript down!"

Lynn Moen, for suggesting the first part of the title.

Niles Newton, for her true interest, her many helpful suggestions and materials, and her encouraging statement, "A book such as this is much needed in our society."

I also wish to thank Hazel Turner, Barb Wandrei, Robert Genovese, Reynold Mattson, Lucy Cutler, the LLLI Founding Mothers, and the many parents who participated in the questionnaires.

Foreword

Were modern society thriving with high level wellness at all ages and stages of life, physicians and others interested in childrearing would have a right to dismiss a book promoting the old-fashioned notion that the parental bed be converted into a family bed. With modern society, however, suffering from a marked dysfunctioning and harboring doubts that there will be a viable society to turn over to the next generation, we can afford to be open minded about a practice which purports to contribute to the emotional security of a human being.

The indices of a sick society—alienation and psychiatric illness, suicide attempts and suicide, alcoholism and drug misuse, infidelity and divorce, pornography and perversion, sexual restlessness and impotency, juvenile delinquency, child abuse and violent crime—have been steadily rising since World War I. Psychiatry, for the most part, has responded remedially and ineffectively: at the technologic level with shock therapy, frontal lobotomies and psychopharmaceuticals (billions of dollars are now spent on tranquilizers); at the psychologic level with an unawareness or insensitivity to nurturent needs and with a permissiveness which, severed from controlling social norms, reflects an excessive counter-reaction to a preceding Victorian age.

Unfortunately, today's mental health movement is a movement primarily concerned with the management of mental illness, not with the promotion of mental health, the latter being hardly more than a platitudinous window-dressing. Physicians in general, and psychiatrists in particular (neither of whom are especially competent in their own family life or even partially immune from personal psychiatric problems), preoccupied with patient problems and lulled by the blandishments of drug companies and the ready promises of the prescription pad, fail to reflect on and explore the true nature of a mental health movement—one directed to the preservation, promotion and perfection of the initial mental health with which man is endowed at birth.

For though nature turns over to us more than three million babies a year, virtually all of whom are psychologically healthy, the fact is that the majority of them, despite continuing medical attendance (or because of it), grow up emotionally insecure, and one out of ten newborns enters a mental institution sometime in the course of his or her lifetime. Now, especially that it is becoming virtually impossible to supply enough psychiatrists, psychiatric social workers, nurses, and psychiatric facilities to handle the mounting number of patients needing help, it would seem that society should turn its attention to the earlier years to see when and how things went wrong. It is perhaps our only hope for stemming the tide of psychiatrically crippled human beings.

What we must be mindful of if we have any respect for nature is that she has accumulated a built-in wisdom born of a vast clinical experience over millions of years, out of which a reciprocal fitness between the living thing and its environment has evolved. In mammalia this is found particularly in the intimate relationship of mother and young. The mother is nature's 'prepared environment' for the newborn! We cannot afford to ignore this wisdom. Literally this is what the natural sciences are about: to discover the wisdom of nature; that is, the laws, nuances and subtleties of nature which enabled our species to survive and prosper. In the meantime, to bridge the gap between what we already know (or think we know) and what we have yet to learn—what is yet to be discovered by the activities of countless researchers in thousands of laboratories—the prudent and sagacious man must seek his cues and clues and norms from the operations of nature. Here we must remember that medicine, in its broadest sense, is a normative art.

The fatal mistake we have made in medicine, not only in psychiatry but even more so in pediatrics and obstetrics, was to introduce practices which deviated from normal physiologic and psychologic processes without first firmly researching the full implications and wisdom of man-imposed changes. This is best exemplified by the ignorance inherent in the ready substitution of bottle feeding for breastfeeding as if, to recall Oliver Wendell Holmes, the two hemispheres of the contemporary pediatrician's brain is superior to a pair of mammary glands in the art of compounding a nutritive fluid for infants. We forget that the root of the word *physician* is *phusis* which means nature, and that medicine is a cooperative art because it cooperates with the active mechanisms of nature and the goal of nature which it shares. (The same mistake is also seen by our having made the drugged and operative hospital delivery the prevalent as opposed to the natural delivery.)

The fitness of the environment for the living, whose fitness is reciprocal to the environment, is not only a matter of the physical, such as water, oxygen, nitrogen, carbon and trace minerals, but also of the psychologic, as seen by the maternal and parental environment without which the young of mammalia cannot survive or emotionally mature. Here it must be stressed that it is the family, not the individual, which is the proper unit of care, because the family, especially as it concerns the psyche, is the maker or breaker of health.

The fact that modern medicine and technology, despite its many brilliant accomplishments, has not given society high, or even low, level wellness (nor has the huge amount of money we have expended, as if health were a commodity that could be bought in the market place —see *Child & Family.* 7: 73–74, 1968) nor even slowed up the prevailing malaise that is enveloping our country should make us reconsider our problem and its solution.

Accordingly, it is incumbent upon the reader, particularly those who are professionals in the medical and behavioral sciences, to approach *The Family Bed* with an open mind. It cogently brings to life the manner in which a family functions or may function in attaining its purpose—the giving of mature adults to society at large. Enough studies now exist to document with finality that the first years of life are vital if not crucial to adult maturity; that the indices of a sick society are symptomatic manifestations in later life of insecurities generated in earlier years. Even academia—the Harvard studies under Dr. Burton White—reaffirm the importance of full-time attention of a mother (or a mother substitute) to the dependent child in his or her first two or three years of life for the child's optimal emotional development. The time is long overdue for parents, physicians, social agencies and government experts to realize that they have been working at the wrong end of the age scale in seeking basic solutions. We must recognize that the dysfunctioning family should be corrected and helped to function properly in its work as the prime health maker for society.

The Family Bed is a case in point. The author's thesis is that there is something natural, right and salutary in the desire of young children to convert the parental bed into a family bed. The exposition of her thesis is substantial. In fact, it is as if Maria Montessori whispered in her ear, "If you want to understand the needs of children, observe and study the child." That very young children, always and everywhere—in contrast to older children—prefer the family bed to their own bed or their own room communicates a convincing message. Since man is not only a social animal but a gregarious animal as well, the ramifications of interfering with such a universal, inborn natural inclination may be extensive.

One of the great strengths of The Family Bed stems from the author's recognition of the experience and convictions of mothers who accept rather than reject motherhood as a vocation and who make a point of trying to enrich their vocation by participating in mothering organizations such as La Leche League International. Many of these mothers have large families, mothers whom Sir James Spence characterized as really good at motherhood. (The Purpose of the Family. Child and Family. 7:328. 1968). Such mothers, practitioners as opposed to theorists, are the real experts. They contrast to the Spocks and Salks, who, when they are right, are simply echoes of what the good mother has learned by being attentive and responsive to the voice of nature. Profundity characterizes the simple conclusion of a mother that "Babies wants and needs are one and the same thing"; or of another, "Society has taken away the right of a baby to be dependent upon his mother."

The Family Bed is most readable. It will bring joy and support to parents who refuse to reject the silent (and sometimes not so silent) importunings of their children and who refuse to banish them to isolated, solitary outposts. It will help other parents take a second look at what parenthood is all about. Parents tell me that the best advice I gave them as young couples entering marriage and parenthood was first, to invest in a king-size bed, and second, to never forget that the fastest road to furthering independence in their children is total attention to the needs of their children in their dependent years.

Herbert Ratner, M.D., Editor
Child & Family Quarterly

Preface

During my pregnancy with my first child, several people approached me with the suggestion that I attend La Leche League (LLL) meetings. There, I was told, I would learn all about breastfeeding and nurturing my baby. I thanked them politely but inwardly stuck up my nose with a bit of arrogance and thought to myself, "I don't need their advice. I'm from the old country and know all there is to know about taking care of a child."

My baby girl was six weeks old when, one lonely, tearful night, I found myself sitting with her in the rocking chair, bottle in one hand, pacifier in the other, agonizing about what I was doing wrong. The following day I called LLL. As time went on, a comfortable, successful nursing relationship was established and all seemed well, except for one thing. Yvonne needed to be held so much and would not go to sleep by herself. Many a doubtful, stressful night was spent at her bedside. Unfortunately, this time I had no one to call upon. No books, no organization. In the early '70's even LLL had no clear answer. My heritage did not help me much, either. The "let her cry it out" method seemed totally contrary to my maternal feelings.

I discovered other parents with similar problems. After many inquiries, however, it became apparent that one particular answer surfaced time and again from those parents who seemed to have fairly peaceful bed and nighttime hours with their children. What was their secret? I asked and received the answer; a loving and simple one. An answer strangely foreign to our Western culture, and yet one that made so much sense: "We take the child to bed with us."

Would others want to hear this solution? As I began working on the manuscript, word about my writing spread and I received urgent pleas from parents all over the world. "Please send us a copy of your book. We are having so many sleep problems with our child."

The book sold quickly. The same desperate parents who had cried for help now wrote, "Thank God, now I can finally do what I have always felt was the right thing to do. We have no more going-to-sleep problems and everyone is happier."

It made no difference whether their profession was homemaker, psychiatrist, child educator, or office worker—all seemed relieved to know that it was really quite all right to lovingly and closely nurture a child at night as well as during the day. They discovered with surprise what so many other cultures around the world take for granted. Even so, to avoid admonition, negative peer pressure, or a downright fierce guilt-trip dumped upon them by "others," these parents may still whisper behind their hand, "If you don't tell anyone, this is what we do. ..." This book shares with everyone interested in preventing or solving bed or nighttime problems the secret that was passed on to me by thousands of parents.

This is an age when men value organizations more than their members. When we force children to conform to our convenience, our schedules, our boundaries, and our locked doors, we show them that we value the system more than we value them.

Dr. James Clark Moloney

1

A Rediscovery

Our days, our deeds, all we achieve or are
Lie folded in our infancy.

John T. Trowbridge

Most of us have read or heard, at one time or another, an "Authority's" advice on children sleeping with their parents or with other siblings. Although opinions on this subject are quite controversial, the practice is usually frowned upon. This is because such persons, by nature of their professions, usually follow what they have been taught in school. Also, they are frequently associated only in contact with troubled cases that were brought to them because of a need for professional attention. When co-family sleeping *is* "permitted," it is usually not without the child care practitioner's own personal opinion as to what extent and with what limitations it should be followed. Of course, personal opinions differ tremendously and, being personal, often have nothing to do with fact or even reality. They may change as the practitioner's exposure to co-family sleeping expands. The professionals who are most likely to advocate a relaxed, loving family sleeping situation are those who have themselves experienced such a sleeping set-up, discovering that it does not lead to dire consequences. Slowly but surely we are beginning to hear from these doctors, while others are venturing to open their minds.

In a 1979 June issue of *Redbook,* Dr. T. Berry Brazelton made a revealing statement for which I have high respect. He felt he had to re-evaluate his rather rigid ideas on handling sleep problems in our culture. Dr. Brazelton had received an overwhelming number of letters from parents across the country who disagreed with his advice that children should not sleep in the same bed as their parents. What he did not realize was how many parents "did not believe in helping a child learn to sleep alone at night."

1

On the other hand, one can pick up many a book on child rearing and read that bad sleeping habits in a child are formed when Mother hears Baby whimper and "rushes" in to see if everything is all right. According to these books, the child will wake up more frequently just to receive his mother's attention. "They will wrap you around their little finger," so take heed. Yet, this seems such a distrustful approach to take toward an innocent baby, who simply needs care and love. Mother is reprimanded for wanting to pick up her crying baby. Yet responding to Baby's call shows concern for her child, and is an action that comes from the very heart of motherhood.

The child, meanwhile, is scolded for reaching out to his parents during a time of need. He is to be told "lovingly" but firmly that night is not a time for parental love and attention. "Now go to sleep," his mother says. Can anyone "go to sleep" upon command, especially during a time of loneliness or fright? Such books strongly advise parents not to take their children to bed with them, whether in time of stress or as a matter of course. The parent is neither allowed nor encouraged to place trust in his own parental emotions. Instead, he becomes the innocent victim of social taboos that seem to change with every generation. Every few years a new book on child rearing floods the market and confuses the issue, but all claim to have "the answer" to ideal child rearing, as seen from the perch of an armchair. My great-grandmother was told to nurse her baby every three hours throughout the day. Start solids at nine months. Baby should sleep a predetermined number of hours during the day, as well as at night.

My mother was encouraged to bottlefeed her children, and only every four hours. Start solids at six months. A crying baby was not to be picked up until it was "time". Baby slept in his own crib or bassinet. When my babies were born, breastfeeding was actually discouraged as not being very scientific. Solid food was introduced at three to six weeks. Babies must sleep in their own rooms. The big problem was that my children did not read those books, did not understand clocks and schedules, and challenged all those man-made introductions. This book is a result of the search for child rearing methods that would work for me and my children. And after seventeen years I can honestly say that they have worked beautifully: nursing on demand, weaning when ready, sleeping when tired and wherever the baby happened to be, and co-family sleeping until each child wanted a room of her own. Approach: Listen to the child.

Society tells us that co-family sleeping is taboo. But it doesn't give us any satisfactory answers to bed and nighttime problems with children, either.

The parental instinct should not be underestimated, although this seemed to be the trend for many years. But times began to change in the '70's. In a 1974 newspaper article, Dr. Spock said that parents of this country are convinced that only trained persons know how children should be reared. This, he continued, has resulted in a lack of self-assurance on the part of parents. He goes so far as to call it a "cruel deprivation" that has been imposed on mothers and fathers.

In 1974, another article appeared entitled "Why Some Babies Don't Sleep." (*English Journal.* "New Society"). The authors of this article found that the most common problem of parental concern was the child's waking at night. In their comments on the result of their research, they wrote that some of the advice that frequently comes from health visitors, welfare clinics, and general practitioners is not always very helpful and may actually have little real experience behind it. The minimum research that is done on this problem, compared with matters concerning hospital care of sick babies is, as a matter of fact, striking. "What has emerged from the research," they continue, "has not filtered through very effectively to those who need it."

What do parents have to say on this subject? One young mother wrote, "I deeply feel that our baby should be with us during the night. However, she has a bedroom of her own. Why? I do not know. I wish it could be different. We frequently have such difficulty in getting her to sleep without crying. I wish I knew what to do."

I was this mother, writing about our first child when she was nine months old. As a new parent, it never occurred to me then to take her into bed with my husband and me.

By the time our second child was born, we had talked about this subject with many people. To our great surprise, we found many who "confessed" to taking their children into bed with them. They did so usually because of a child's sleeping problem or because it seemed to result in a happier family.

It is amazing that something as natural, loving, and comforting as co-family sleeping should even be a subject for discussion. But, alas, it is not the first, natural thing that has been disrupted by scientific intervention. Cribs, clocks, and multiple-room dwellings where several rooms are specifically set aside for an individual's sleeping—all come under the heading of inventions. And an invention is on precarious ground because it is often not in harmony with nature. It is "new and improved." The ingredients for love and a closeknit family life, however, have only to be rediscovered. They have been there all along.

A great majority of successful breastfeeding mothers take their babies to bed with them. Since comparatively few mothers breastfeed for any length of time in our culture, it is no wonder that family bed sharing is not the norm. Many parents have never even heard of it, let alone considered it. In cultures where breastfeeding is the norm, bed sharing is frequently as familiar as the family dinner table in our own culture. According to a study by Dr. Niles Newton, which compared the behavior of nursing and non-nursing mothers, there is a significant difference in willingness to share a bed with their babies. Women who breastfeed their children appear to be less concerned with current cultural disapproval of bed sharing.[1]

This, then, also explains why so many parents said that La Leche League, an organization that helps mothers with the art of breastfeeding, specifically helped them to realize the benefits of having their young children sleep with them.

I would like to emphasize that this book does not quote statistics. It does not intend to "prove" anything. It provides insight, encouragement, and a reason for co-family sleeping. Primarily, it supports the opinion that an open door policy to the family bed is an integral part of open communication and listening to the child's need. This does not mean that everyone must hop into one bed, nor that one is a less than good parent if his children sleep in their own bed. *The Family Bed* is a concept, part of a total picture, one step toward rearing happy children. The book releases families from the social taboo and gives them a freedom of choice.

It should be mentioned that no specific age of the child has been given. He may be referred to as a baby, young child, or child. This has been done to alleviate the strong influence a prescribed age has on a child's expected accomplishments. Most children, for instance, are no longer afraid of the dark by the time they are twelve years old. But suppose you have a child who is thirteen and still expresses fear? There really isn't much you can do about it, except love him, accept him, work with him, and wait until he is no longer afraid.

Among children who are accustomed to sleeping with someone from birth on, there seems to be a natural graduation from needing to sleep in the parental bed to sleeping with other siblings. This book's emphasis is on the young child. It is to be recognized, therefore, that when I speak of sleeping together, i.e. co-family sleeping, the implication is sleeping with whomever he chooses, according to his emotional development. Thus, some children are ready to leave the family bed at age two, while others may not be ready until a much later age.

Twenty-five years ago, when prepared or natural childbirth was a "new" idea, little information was available on the subject. Many people, doctors and laymen alike, scoffed at the concept. Today, because the medical profession and mothers have found it acceptable for the mother to be awake and aware during her labor and birth, prepared childbirth is no longer a novelty. It is becoming quite common, and proving to be highly beneficial and effective.

"IT'S EASY FOR YOU TO SAY, 'DON'T BE AFRAID OF THE DARK'...
...YOU GOT SOMEBODY TO SLEEP WITH!"

Likewise, breastfeeding has made a comeback. There is now "scientific proof" that nursing at the breast is superior to any other infant feeding method. During the last twenty years, an increasing number of publications on the great advantages of breastfeeding have been appearing on the market.

So, also, co-family sleeping is a relatively new idea—new, that is, since we got away from it a mere century ago. Before this natural behavior will again become accepted, its importance and benefits too will have to be proven scientifically. Thirty years ago it might have been difficult to obtain sufficient convincing evidence. Thirty years ago this book might have had little support. Today, a growing amount of research on the negative results of separation of a mother and her child is becoming available and accepted. Bowlby's book *Separation*, volume two of *Attachment and Loss*, goes into the greatest detail describing the effects on a child when he is prematurely separated from his mother. The author, who is a world authority on maternal attachment and deprivation, discusses in great length the possible psychopathic results of such separation. However, he has simply researched and documented what any keen observer could have realized: unnecessary and prematurely-enforced separation does not make a child happy. It is the author's feeling that a happy child is a secure child.

A mother went on to say that she has always known that a baby is much happier while being held. "But nobody ever gave me a grant to publish that fact." She concluded that, "When I need advice on rearing children, I always ask experienced mothers and fathers of loving children."

Bottles and formula, cribs and clocks, and night lights are inventions that have been tried on children over the past several short centuries. In the meantime, Mother's milk and Mother's arms have always been available, patiently waiting for the passing of man's foolhardy arrogance, which tried to convince us that his inventions were superior to nature. But just wait a minute. Science is now "proving" that which many a parent's heart has known for years: "My child needs me at night as well as during the day and holding him makes him a more secure and happier person."

2

It Was Meant To Be

The home we first knew on this beautiful earth,
The friends of our childhood, the place of our birth,
In the hearts' inner chamber sung always will be,
As the shell ever sings of its home in the sea.

Francis Dana Gage, *Home*

It is quiet. It is dark. It is night. Somewhere a baby whimpers. His mother stirs and pulls her infant toward her. He nuzzles for her breast. He begins to nurse and both Mother and Baby fall back to sleep. Somewhere in his dream Papa knows all is well. All are asleep.

Somewhere a toddler awakens, and sleepily cries, "Mama?" Mama stirs in her sleep, reaches over and takes the child's hand in her hand. They both fall back to sleep. Papa's dreams were not even interrupted. All is well. All are asleep.

Whether it be on a Japanese "futon," or under an arctic caribou skin, on the bare African ground, in a large four-poster bed, or in a double-twin size bed, whether they be poor or rich, large or small, families all over the world sleep together, and have done so since the beginning of mankind.

Separate sleeping is mainly a western culture custom and, as social customs go, they change with the times. The Western world has seen a hundred years or so in which separate sleeping has been strongly advocated; so strongly, as a matter of fact, that many parents feel guilty in taking their children to bed with them. However, the time has come when parents are not necessarily satisfied with doing things the way their parents did them. They are questioning doing "as they are told," especially when it produces tension, unhappiness, and unhealthy situations.

Modern parents are seeking fulfillment, which they perhaps instinctively feel has been lacking. A mother, pregnant for the second time,

7

hesitantly agrees to attend prepared childbirth classes. Her first birth, an experience in which she was unable to participate as fully as possible, has left her with vague, dissatisfied memories. The second birth is beautiful. She has prepared herself and is awake and aware when her child is born. A bottlefeeding mother decides to breastfeed...after all, it was meant to be. What a glorious experience! What closeness! "No," she says, "I'll not let you be taken away from me and put into another bed, in another room. We belong together." Mother and Baby nestle close in bed. Father puts his arm around the two. Then they fall asleep. It, too, was meant to be.

Perhaps this may all sound rather idealistic to those who have never experienced sleeping peacefully with their children. But it is not so, as parents will testify throughout this book.

There are those who have never read much about child rearing. They just do what comes naturally. "We allowed our child to sleep with us because we just felt it was the easiest, most natural thing to do," a young couple wrote. "In fact, we had never even thought about it as being different until we mentioned it to other people."

In trying to understand their children's needs, it has been helpful for parents to recall their own childhood, when they would seek refuge in their parents' bed during stressful times. It felt so safe and reassuring.

Even lying down with them until they fall asleep is not enough for some children. Parents sadly remember not being allowed into their parents' bed. "I was never allowed in my parents' bed," writes a young mother. "I can remember many nights feeling tremendously frightened and lonely, but knowing that I really shouldn't go and wake them. Sometimes my mother or father would come into my room and lie down with me, but it was just not the same. All the while I knew that they'd leave as soon as I had fallen asleep. I never want our children to feel unwelcome."

But those parents who did experience family sleeping in their young years remember it fondly. "I slept with my parents off and on until I was eight years old. So did my brother. My mother now sleeps with her grandchildren on every occasion she has. She says it brings back memories of the time when we were little. We are still a closeknit and loving family. P.S. If a mom or dad were not available to climb into bed with, a brother, aunt, or grandparent would always oblige willingly."

Most parents wrote that with their first-born they started sleeping arrangements in the conventional way; separate bedrooms for the child and no permission for him to come into bed with them. But slowly, with each additional child, they changed their views and began favoring co-family sleeping.

"With our first child, I was much more concerned with 'high' child rearing ideals," a father of two children wrote to me. "We became more relaxed with our second one. The benefits showed on the first child also."

One mother found it impossible, with her fifth child, to get in and out of bed at night in order to cater to him, and still assure herself of proper rest. When the infant was a few weeks old, Mother was so exhausted that she took Baby to bed with her. They stayed there until morning. She found that her infant slept longer and better and she could doze even while breastfeeding him. The arrangement was so satisfactory that it became permanent for the next three years. The other children, too, occasionally joined them in bed. She commented, "I could now cope better with being a wife and mother. As a result my husband was also happier."

Parents found that children awakened in a much more pleasant mood than when they had slept alone in their own bed. "They wake up with a smile," wrote one mother. "We feel that children were meant to sleep with their parents."

Several parents expressed the opinion that since their family began to sleep together, its members were more relaxed, touched one another more, and felt closer to each other. One mother, realizing the importance of touch, wrote, "Our family does not 'touch' physically as much as I would like. Night contact is one way of making up for this."

The following letter from a mother sums it up nicely:

> As an educated member of our culture, having studied child development in college and having applied the research skills acquired in studying for a Ph.D. in literature to such other important areas of my life as child rearing, I was firmly convinced of the lack of wisdom and just plain ignorance involved in allowing children in the parental bed. My first child was a hyperkinetic infant whose only comfort was constant body contact. It also turned out later that he suffered from poor eyesight and therefore had not been able to be reassured by the sight of me, but

only by touch. He slept a total of eight hours in twenty-four, but in such short snatches that I got only three. We spent about fourteen hours a day in the rocking chair. I would get him to sleep, and lay him down in his cradle ever so carefully, only to see him go into a startle reaction as soon as he touched the mattress. Even gently warming his cradle with a low-setting heating pad, which I would remove to lay him down in the warm place, didn't help. Now my instinct cried out to let him sleep on me while I was in a place and position where I could sleep also. But no, I "knew" that this was unwise, even dangerous. I learned the meaning of the word "zombie"; a body with no soul in it. Mechanically I stumbled through the endless round of day and night, unable to concentrate on a single coherent thought. My baby and I cried together in that old rocking chair. Finally, when he was seven and a half months old, I put his crib in the living room, shut the bedroom door, put on the noisy old air conditioner, and let him cry it out. He never "learned" to sleep through the night. But he did learn that he couldn't expect his mother's comfort and care for one-third of every twenty-four hour period. I was desperate, but I have desperately regretted it since.

Because I had been unsuccessful nursing him, I went to La Leche League during my second pregnancy. With fascination I learned that there were women who let their babies sleep with them! I questioned them eagerly about their experiences. I observed their older children, all apparently psychologically healthy and more emotionally independent than my own five-year-old. No one had experienced marital strain as a result, but rather the contrary. To my query, "If you start them off in your bed, aren't you afraid they'll never want to sleep in their own?" I received the reply, "If you start them off in diapers, aren't you afraid they'll never want to use the toilet?" Maturation, of course, was the key to this, as in all things.

So my daughter slept with me from the moment she came home from the hospital. How easy it all was! It took only eight and a half hours in bed to get eight hours worth of sleep, even though she nursed seven or eight times during the night. When our five-year-old found out that the baby was sleeping with us, he wanted to, also. We made him welcome, and found that a great deal of his night agitation quieted immediately. He still woke up, but was able to return to sleep much more easily. After about a year of this, his night need for us dramatically decreased. And he never experienced the nightmare phase so common in our culture, which I vividly remember from my own childhood.

My deepest sorrow is that I allowed my mothering instincts (to keep my baby in bed with me) to become "educated" out of me, and that I was physically and emotionally unable to meet his needs for nurturance and body contact as a result. We teach our children right from infancy to turn to things (blanket, teddy bear, pacifier) instead of people for comfort. Then we wonder why we are a materialistic society!

The major reason why parents will not allow their children to sleep with them seems mainly parent-oriented. Those who are in favor, however, give both parent-oriented reasons—"It was easier. We enjoy it," as well as child-oriented ones—"Because my child seemed to need it."

Following is a list of reasons why parents have their children sleep with them:

- Incidence of night problems, teething, bad dreams. (Bad dreams, incidentally, were mentioned very frequently.)
- We feel Baby needs twenty-four hour continuous closeness with Mother.
- When we are in strange surroundings, it acts as a form of security.
- To relax the child and get him off to sleep.
- From exhaustion—being up at night.
- Too cold to get up at night to tend to Baby.
- We enjoyed the closeness, and like snuggling with him.
- When we feel especially close to him.
- It just happened over the years.
- Due to limited amount of heat during the night.
- Because of emotional benefits.
- As a method of child spacing. Since Baby could nurse freely at night, it helped to suppress ovulation.
- This way we were always aware of his well-being.
- We truly had the feeling that he belonged to us, that we were all one big family.
- Husband thought the baby looked lonely.
- It fulfills my protective and mothering instinct.
- It is easier when I (the mother) am ill.
- It is easier when a child is ill.
- Because husband and children want it.
- Because of memories of my own childhood.

- We enjoy the quiet time together with one or more children.
- At 2 a.m. I'm too tired to object.
- Lack of sleeping places.
- It is the easiest way to keep the children quiet and get them off to sleep.

Contrary to those who bemoan not having enough room to stretch out when children are in their bed, some parents take it all in stride. They emphasize the positive qualities. "I often think, as I lie 'squished' between my dear husband and our two- or four-year-old, 'I am such a lucky woman to be so close to the people I love so very much.'"

The family that is accustomed to sleeping together finds camping no problem at all. Similarly, overnight stays at a relative's home are no trouble at all, or if for some reason the family has to bundle together for lack of space or beds.

One mother wrote, "We enjoy having our friends stay overnight. There is no fuss or worry about where Baby sleeps. Of course he sleeps with Mom and Dad. There is no need for a crib or playpen, swing or infant seat, or any of the other gadgets that serve as a mother substitute. If people only knew how simple mothering can be! One Mother, one Baby, one Dad, maybe a baby carrier, some nice warm convenient breast milk, a dry diaper, and life is easy and relaxed. I love to be cuddly and warm. Don't you? Why not let the rest of the family enjoy this wonderful closeness?"

The parental bed seems to be a focal point for activities other than sleeping. Parents have noticed that their children like to read, play games, or just lounge on their bed. Pre-schoolers take naps more easily, and one mother even felt that sick children become well more quickly! It is a beautiful cure-all.

The parents of a deaf child wrote: "One difference we have noticed when talking to other parents of deaf children is the minimum behavior and frustration problems our son has compared to other deaf children. Temper tantrums without reason are usually kept at a minimum, and people cannot understand that he is deaf because he is so 'normal'." Another father commented that the instructors at the center that his eighteen-month-old deaf and blind son attends have repeatedly attested to the child's confident behavior. From birth on the child was breastfed, carried around a great deal, and allowed to sleep with his parents. His handicap was not discovered until he was a few months old.

In the book, *In This Sign*, by Joanne Greenberg, the young mother Janice slept with one hand upon her newborn baby. Janice is a deaf-mute mother. She would awaken when she felt her baby begin to cry.

Karen Pryor, author of *Nursing Your Baby*, notes especially how beneficial it is for a child with neurological difficulties to sleep with his mother.

One of the most laudable aspects of a person's child rearing ways is his ability to place his highest value in the child rather than in things. This form of maturity takes time, however. Not infrequently, several children have entered the family before a parent has grown into this realization. It takes time and growing along with the children to be able to balance the influence of clocks, social opinions, and material objects with the needs of our children. We become more relaxed about certain aspects of child rearing and family living. We realize that book theories cannot usually be applied verbatim to our highly individual children.

"How can you be consistent?" asked a father. "They never do the same thing twice!" And a scholar in child rearing education admitted that while still in college he lectured on the topic, "Twelve *requirements* in rearing children." After his schooling he married and had several children of his own. After a few years he realized that the topic of his lectures needed some change. It was now entitled, "Twelve *suggestions* in rearing children." When his children reached their teens, he decided, much to his chagrin, that he needed to change the title once again. This time he came up with, "Twelve *hints* in rearing children."

As we look back in our child rearing years we often sigh and say, "If I could do it over again . . ." So it is with sleeping arrangements. "I wish," wrote one parent, "we could have had a king-size bed when we were first married. It would have helped a lot. If I could do it all over again, I'd like to have two or three mattresses on the floor so everyone could sleep together until the children wanted to have their own room or bed. I'm sure that before too long some of our children will want privacy, but until that time I want them to feel welcome in our bed."

Another parent admits, "We changed the sleeping arrangements from separate to all-together with our third and fourth children. We grew up, matured, and changed our values from things to people."

Other parents mentioned how they became less self-centered, self-interested. A mother told me, "I used to tell my little two-year-old, 'I need my sleep, too. You are in the way when you sleep with me.' Now, two children later, I realize that once I shifted the interest in myself to my children, many of the inconveniences that irritated me and were so overbearing diminished in importance."

Quite a few parents have referred to themselves as being "dumb," "stupid," "immature," or "too self-centered," in refusing their first few children their bed. Once they allowed the children with them they felt more mature, fulfilled, wiser, more understanding of the needs of others.

I consider it noteworthy that I know of no families who have reversed their sleeping habits from co-family sleeping on a regular basis to separate sleeping. When co-family sleeping was necessary, such as on a vacation trip, then yes, some parents could not wait to sleep by themselves again. But when it involved a growing understanding of the children's needs, the change to co-family sleeping also seemed to grow in acceptance.

What wonderful memories from these child-filled years we will have to treasure for the rest of our lives. Anyone who has ever awakened in the morning to find his little child curled up against him, sleeping so peacefully, knows what I mean when I say I'm convinced that this must be the right thing to do.

There is nothing more precious, nothing that can compare.

I remember being awakened one night by my little girl, who had not yet weaned. She had been sleeping against my back when she sat up, peeked over, and joyfully exclaimed, "There it is." She swung over, nestled against me, and began to nurse contentedly. We both fell asleep again (myself, giggling.)

We were meant to bring forth children in love and happiness. If your child is unhappy, you will be unhappy. If your child is full of laughter, you will be the happiest person. Children love to be with people. Let's make them happy and have them sleep with their parents or brothers and sisters. After all, it was really meant to be this way. How do we know? Ask a happy child who was allowed to sleep with another human being. Ask a happy mother who has experienced the tenderness of her sleeping child snuggled next to her in bed.

Mrs. W., who has six children, ages fourteen months to nineteen years, tells us:

> The very first time we had a child in our bed was when our first-born was about eighteen months and big enough to climb out of his crib.

We were too sleepy that night to be analytical of the child-in-bed-with-parents situation, so we welcomed him, along with a big stuffed animal. The following day I fixed his crib so he couldn't get hurt if he climbed out. He continued to come to our bed from then on. Sometimes he would come for several nights in succession. At other times he would come in only occasionally.

Our second child exhibited fear of noises, the wind, and the dark. As soon as she could get out of her crib, she too came to our bed frequently at night. However, she came less often than our first child because she shared a room with her big brother. This, in itself, seemed to lessen her fears. Sometimes, instead of coming to us, she crawled into bed with her brother.

Our third and fourth children followed much the same pattern: as soon as they were able, they went leaping over the crib side and into bed with a sibling. These two preferred their siblings' beds to that of the master bed. When they outgrew their cribs, we invested in two double beds and put our four children together.

The real rooming-in began with our fifth child. With four other children to care for during the daytime hours, and a job to uphold, it was imperative that Mother and Father get their sleep at night. After four weeks of being up at all hours with my newborn, I discovered that everyone could get a lot more sleep when Baby slept with me. Sometimes, if Baby had a restless night, Father resorted to sleeping elsewhere in the house. This is certainly a small inconvenience for the larger gain of everyone's getting their necessary rest. The child nursed frequently at night during his first year and into the second and third years.

When "Baby" was three years old, we felt that he should have his own bed, at least for purposes of identity if not for every night occupancy. He liked the idea. I nursed him in the living room or bedroom before tucking him in. Having contented himself at the breast, he then went up to bed. Sometimes he chose to sleep with his parents or siblings instead of in his own bed. Whenever Daddy was working nights, this youngest child knew that there was an empty slot next to me. So he usually claimed it, although by this time our third and fourth children had become interested in sleeping with us and asked to take turns. Our household had quite a flexible sleeping arrangement.

Just before the youngest's fourth birthday, we had our sixth child. For the first time in our childbearing years there was not a crib in the house. It was assumed that Baby Raphael would sleep with us until he asked for a bed of his own. Our older children still want to sleep with us sometimes. Perhaps this is mainly because they like to be near the baby. A mattress placed alongside the bed holds any and all who want to join us. Somehow that mattress has come to be called the "clubhouse," which is, by definition, a place where friends with a common purpose meet and communicate.

During the past year my husband's work has required him to get up at five a.m. In order not to awaken the sleeping herd, he chooses to sleep in another room on his working nights.

In summary, I would describe our sleeping situation as subject to variation. Neither spouse feels threatened by the children's need for their parents during the night. We see nighttime needs as important as daytime needs. As our family has grown in size and age, the once typical, much talked about, connubial chamber has certainly undergone some changes. These changes, we are convinced, are for the best. Whatever inconveniences or disappointments we might have faced, the end product is completely satisfying.

My answer to that tired old question, how do you have sexual relations with children nearby, is, "without fanfare and when it is convenient." A more serious question might be, do you disturb one another when everyone sleeps so close together? My reply is "sometimes, but surely not always." Our sleep is also disturbed by loud neighbors, the telephone, airplanes, sirens, etc. We feel that our own children are the least of any disturbances that occur during sleep.

One last parting thought. Last week our nine-year-old awakened ill, and it was decided that he should stay home from school for the day. Without any previous comment he left his own bed, brought his get-well equipment with him, and set up shop in our bed. He probably would have recovered in any other bed or room. But his choice of quarters for healing purposes was interesting to observe.

Mrs. O., who has eight children, ages four to eighteen years, tells us:

Our first four children were born before we became familiar with La Leche League philosophies. They slept in cribs away from our bedroom.

When La Leche League came into our life, my husband was delighted to hear that it was all right to have the children sleep with us. It was not so with me! I didn't like to sleep like a pretzel. I liked to sleep cuddled next to my husband, not with a baby between us. But gradually, as he insisted, I saw the wisdom behind this "new" idea. Our fifth baby loved it, and I discovered a definite new response in this baby that had not been evident in the other four children. I had always wanted to hug and cuddle our babies, but they squirmed and seemed to be very independent. They did not respond as I thought babies should. But this baby loved to touch, caress, and stroke me, and she wanted this in return. An emotional closeness was developing between us, which had been missing with the older children.

I watched our fifth baby in her sleep and observed that she always slept with at least one part of her body touching either me or my husband. If she stirred and lost this contact, she would grope around— still in her sleep—until she touched skin again. She would then relax and lie contentedly. She continued to sleep with us until she was old enough to sleep in the bottom part of a bunk bed.

When Joe, our sixth child, was born, he also slept with us. (Now eight years old, he is still a regular partner in our bed.) Two years after Joe, our seventh child was born. By this time our bed was getting crowded. We bought a king-size bed, thinking this would solve the problem. But it only served as an invitation to more of the youngsters. It is now common to have two or three of our eight children sleeping with us. The three oldest ones never do. They were probably too old by the time we opened our bed to the children.

I've tried to analyze why my husband was so eager to have the children sleep with us. He was the seventh child in a family of eight, and he was held a great deal. As a young child, he used to crawl into bed with his mother after Dad went to milk the cows early in the morning. During the early years of our marriage he worked long hours. He missed seeing the children and therefore got into the habit of waking them at eleven p.m. for a short visit.

Now, even though he works from eight a.m. until five p.m., he still remembers those evening hours away from the children. Before they fall asleep, he tells them to come into our bed if they wake during the night. Frequently, three to five of them will fall asleep in our bed. We carry them into their own beds to make room for us.

I've long since discarded my reluctance to have the children in our bed, and I do enjoy their company. The advantages of the real closeness that has developed far outweigh any problems. And we will have precious memories.

Mrs. P., who has seven children, ages nine to twenty-six years, tells us:

We've been married for over thirty years. Our firstborn slept in a crib in our room for only three months. He was then moved to his own room. Our next three babies slept in our room in a crib for at least a year. It was always a comfort for us to be so close to the infant. And it was reassuring that we would be there should he have a need for us.

Our children always chose to sleep with at least one other person. We now have five bedrooms, but even with seven children, two rooms are always empty.

We have told our children that any time they are disturbed or frightened during the night, they can come into our bed. They have always done this. And when any one of them was sick or feverish, my husband or I slept with the sick child. We feel that this extra love made them well much more quickly than medicine could have. We have not had a doctor's bill for nineteen years! God is Love, and we believe that Love heals.

Our last three babies were born at home. It changed our views on many things. My husband discovered new joy in watching the baby sleep next to me so contented at my breast. He strongly felt that Mother and Baby need each other very much and without disturbance during the first few weeks after birth. Baby slept on my tummy a lot during those early weeks.

These last three children, now ages nine, twelve, and fifteen, all slept in our bed from birth until they were about four years old. Then each voluntarily went to his siblings' beds.

Despite what some people may say about the results of this type of dependency on parents, our last three children are very independent and secure in many ways. We can see them all growing up to be loving, caring, and feeling adults. We don't believe this is something one can "teach" a child when he is grown. A child must live with loving adults in order to be able to live this way himself in the future. If people would only stop *talking* about love and *actually love,* there would be a big change in the world.

I remember being at a religious retreat where a young pregnant woman gave a speech on love. (She had left her other young children at home for three days.) I asked her if the new baby would be rooming-in with her at the hospital. She replied, "I want my rest. I will get enough of the bawling brat at home." If this mother can't show love to her own dependent little child, how can she speak on something she doesn't have at home? I believe that true love is that which overflows at home to spill out to others in the world.

Mrs. S., who has five children, ages two to eleven years, tells us:

Many people have commented on the child who always sleeps with his parents. They say that the parents will never get that child out of their bed, so why start something that can't be stopped? They also say you will have no personal life with your husband. In our case, we have found none of these theories to be true.

Our fourth baby was the first to be breastfed and to sleep with us. When she was about six months old she began waking at night. I'd take her to bed so she could nurse, and I usually fell asleep until the morning. As she grew older, she stayed longer, until finally she was with us all night. After several years she slowly began sleeping with her older sisters. She rarely comes to us now.

Our fifth child, age two and a half, has been sleeping with us since we brought her home from the hospital. It was not really planned that way. It all started the first night we came home from the hospital. Before going to bed I nursed her and put her into her crib. She awakened at about two a.m. I took her into our bed then. It was great because we all got the sleep we needed. This became routine. She was a funny little one who would not go to sleep unless I lay down with her on the big bed. So I'd go to sleep too, at about nine p.m., and we'd have a good night's sleep.

We bought a side rail for the bed so that the baby could sleep on the outside of the bed without falling off, and I could sleep next to my husband. Periodically, I would ask my husband if he objected to having the baby in bed with us. I wanted to make sure he knew that I did not prefer the child to him. But he always said he didn't. One week our two-and-a-half-year-old child wanted to sleep with her sister. This she did. My husband then commented that he wasn't sure he was ready to have her leave us.

The joy of having the child in bed with us is that we truly enjoy it also. My husband and I find this our special quiet time together with our baby. We realize that nursing helps a mother to feel close to her baby. We feel that this closeness and an understanding of the child can further develop when the child sleeps with his mother. My husband feels that having the child sleep in the parental bed has helped him, also, to develop a certain closeness and understanding between himself and the child. These feelings have, in turn, been transferred to the older children, who did not sleep with us.

We have found that, if the child is not pushed out of the family bed prematurely, he will voluntarily begin to leave it when he is ready. We feel he is ready when he can be given gentle encouragement to sleep in his own bed or with a brother or sister, and he accepts the change.

My husband and I feel we now have a closer relationship with our children. We only wish that our older children had slept with us. Nevertheless, we feel very fortunate to have had the chance to discover how very special this sleeping arrangement is.

Mrs. A., who has six children, ages two to thirteen years, tells us:

It is morning, and I should feel so happy. Our first-born arrived last night—a good delivery—and he is fine, thank God. But I have a big lump in my throat. If I did have a baby, why isn't he here beside me?

Maybe I'll just call the nursery and see if he's okay. "Of course he's fine," a cool, surprised voice said. Now I just feel foolish for worrying, but the tears are welling in my eyes—and I want to hold him to be sure.

This evening our second child was born, easily and beautifully. I feel so happy but so restless. Maybe I'll walk down to the nursery window and look at her. "What! Are you down here again for the third time? You need your rest—go back to bed and sleep. You can hold her in the morning!" But I'm trying, and sleep won't come. My arms are too empty, and she seems so far away.

We've just had our third child—a big, healthy girl. I'm finally getting used to the routine around here. I am tired. So I'll forget about my baby and get some rest, if I can. (But I wonder why they always take my babies away as though I delivered them only to get rid of them.)

Our fourth baby is here, born a little after midnight on Christmas day. She was the only one I knew in the whole delivery room, and I called out, "I love you"—then felt so foolish amidst all these strangers who smiled. At least this time they've promised me that I can nurse the first day and not wait three days like I had to with the others. Guess I'll just have to reconcile myself to another restless night—why can't I relax like you're supposed to? My heart is overflowing with gratitude for this beautiful Christmas gift, but there's a funny ache there, too—one doesn't loan out her precious gifts right away.

Oh joy of joys—our fifth child has arrived at last, and his Daddy and I shared this glorious time together. Now they want to take our baby away—hospital routine, you know—but we've begged to hold him a while longer. The nurse walked away shaking her head as though we were such stubborn people. Isn't he beautiful—isn't he perfect—isn't our love grand? Oh yes! Imagine, we held him for a whole hour. Time stood still!

Sixth child of ours, you are a treasure, nursing at my breast, cradled in my arms, lying on me, sleeping by my side. Let's etch this calm and peace into memory forever. They say you can't tell where I stop and you begin. I feel so close to God and to all of Creation! It's the Seventh Day, and I'm resting, and All is Good.

All of our birth experiences were happy ones, in that I was awake and aware, heard our babies' first cries, and saw them right after they were born. It's interesting to me, though, that my ways of baby care at home reflected the way in which I was or was not allowed close contact with our babies in the hospital—almost as if I were programmed in a certain direction. (Naturally there were other factors too, such as the changing cultural climate, the reading that I did, and the support and examples of friends.)

With our first child I was more a "thing"-oriented mother. Even breastfeeding was a "business"—ideally, a regulated number of hours apart, a set amount of minutes by the clock at each feeding. It was a ritual of hand and nipple washing, much as I had been taught in the hospital. Lots of baby equipment seemed essential, and when our firstborn was put to sleep in his very large crib and did not seem happy about it, I interpreted his cries as rejection of what we had to offer. (And deep down I felt very inadequate and frustrated as a mother.) But we persevered in trying to keep him sleeping often and long in his crib. I would stand beside him and hold a pacifier in his mouth, trying to get him to fall asleep and stay asleep. Interestingly, at five months he spit the pacifier out and adopted his thumb, which lasted for many years.

In a sense, although I did not let our babies cry without some attention, I literally forced our first ones to "mother" themselves through the long night. I remember well how very tired I was the first few weeks after our first child's birth. I would quickly climb into my own bed whenever I thought he was sleeping. If he awakened soon, I felt resentful at having missed my rest. Having him sleep through the night without a feeding seemed especially important. I pushed for this at seven weeks by offering him his pacifier instead of a feeding when he awakened toward morning. All these devices seem ridiculous to me now. How much easier it would have been for me (and happier for both of us) to have rested and slept together. But at the time this really seemed like a terrible "no-no."

La Leche League entered my life before our fourth child was born. I was allowed to nurse my baby soon after birth. I did relax a lot more at home and breastfed more often and longer. I always rocked and nursed her to sleep. I often fell asleep myself in the rocking chair. She was also the first baby that I carried around in a baby carrier. I began to experience a deep sense of rightness about being this close to my baby. However, it wasn't until our fifth child that I discovered the utter relaxation of nursing *lying down* and the closeness and peace this creates between Mother and Baby. I took many naps with him, and when he would wake up for a while after going to sleep at night, it just seemed the best and most natural thing in the world to bring him to our bed until morning. By the sixth child, I knew and deeply felt that Baby belonged with me day and night. My husband and I just assumed she would spend her waking time close to me and her sleeping time by our side. I look on this interlude as one of the rewards of having children, and am very grateful for having experienced it before it was too late. Not only did it seem to be the right thing to do, it was also very pleasurable and satisfying to have her close to us at night. I feel she knows her Daddy better, too, from sleeping close to him.

Should we have more children, we would continue the pattern that we followed with the last one. Naturally, we regret many of the ways we cared for our first ones and the lonely feelings they must have experienced. I recall with sorrow a lonely little three-year-old trying to come into our bed at night and being hustled immediately back to *his* bed . . . and an unhappy four-year-old being scolded harshly to stay in bed and go to sleep, without any sensitivity on my part as to what was bothering her. But these times are over, and today is what counts most in loving our children. Because of the good experiences we've had with the last babies, I now feel more sensitive to the needs of all our children.

And it is easier to "make up" for a closeness that they missed as babies. Especially at bedtime, such things as backrubs, hugs, kisses, or lying down in their beds and visiting seem very beneficial. I no longer think in terms of "my" bed. If the nine-year-old has a bad dream and wants to lie by us for a while or sleep there that night, it seems right to let her do so. If the two-year-old is still sleeping with us for most of the night, it seems quite okay to have her there, too. All in good time she will wean herself from us and prefer to be with the older ones.

3

Some Parents Hesitate

... it appears to be the fashion these days to disrupt all inherited patterns and to defy in a million small ways what nature seems bent on preserving. *

Kenneth L. Woodward

We enjoy being together when we are eating. We enjoy sitting together on the couch, reading. We enjoy going to church together. We enjoy sitting huddled together around a campfire, singing, talking, reminiscing, or just looking at the dancing flames and listening to the quiet sounds of the night. We enjoy walking together, side by side, or going for a ride, or silently sharing the beauty of a seascape.

We receive encouragement to do all of these things together. The family that plays together, and prays together, will stay together. Yet, when it comes to sleeping together, we bounce headstrong into opposition. Why?

Separate sleeping rooms constitutes a relatively new phenomenon found predominantly in the Western world. But although this custom has a rather large following, it is not without discord. And even though authorities have overwhelmingly cautioned against taking children into the parental bed, parents are doing it—out of need, desperation, or just plain common sense.

This is significant. It indicates that the advice needs considerable re-evaluation. Indeed, the Grand Mere of anthropology, Margaret Mead, in personal correspondence with the author, stated, "The fact that co-family sleeping occurs regularly in many human groups as it does among ours, even though the social code is opposed to this practice, is highly significant, and points to a stubborn human characteristic which is worth following up."

The resulting conflict between nature and social custom is an aspect of child rearing that has, unfortunately, caused much undue frustration and unhappiness. On the one hand, society has made parents feel guilty for fulfilling their child's needs through such things as breastfeeding, weaning late, abundant holding, sleeping with them, answering their cries. Or else parents have felt confused and frustrated because such things were not in fashion and encouragement and information were simply not available. So they agonized and seemed to fly in the face of stern warning, "You will ruin that child."

On the other hand, there is an inner drive in parents that forces them to overlook all this and take in the children anyway. The parents are caught in the middle of two strong forces, the inner and the outer. And who doesn't want to be thought of as a "good" parent?

"This has probably been the most difficult problem we have faced with our child," writes a mother. The child wanted to sleep with his parents. The parents wanted to welcome her, but were afraid of possible harm.

Dr. Lee Salk admits that, even though psychoanalysts have been very firm in their recommendation that parents should *never* allow children into their beds, his experience tells him that very few parents are able to abide by this rule in an absolute fashion.[1] Shouldn't this say something?

If we review literature for parental guidance over the past twenty-five years or so we can find some amazingly unsympathetic advice which, nota bene, changes over the years according to what the current times demand and will tolerate.

A popular pamphlet of 1967, *Infant Care,* distributed freely to new mothers, reads:

> It is a good idea to start the baby out with sleeping arrangements you can keep throughout childhood. This means that you'll expect him to sleep alone, in his own bed. Babies are noisy roommates. You lie awake, waiting for the next gurgle or snort, wondering if he's going to cry or not. It's hard to get the sleep you deserve. Baby finds it pleasant to have you near, and may decide to move in. (*Even the authors of this publication realize that it makes baby happy.* —Author's comment.) He'll do his best to make it a regular thing. And a permanent bedfellow, especially one who is apt to wet the bed, becomes a pest. You're sure to resent it eventually, and the baby will be even more troubled by your refusal to let him in with you.[2]

And thus you are welcomed, precious infant!

Some parents hesitate taking an unhappy child into bed with them because they are convinced that crying can be ignored if there is no apparent reason for it. The routine of schedules and the piteous crying of the infant that goes along with it are all too often considered normal and inevitable. One of the books that attempts to give mothers a picture of what a typical, healthy baby is like describes a usual hospital nursery scene: "He cried hard in the nursery, filling his stomach with gas."[3] Just as it was time for him to be wheeled to his mother for a feeding he had fallen asleep, exhausted.

The author, a doctor, ignores the fact that a crying baby needs relief. Instead, he suggests that the crying is nothing to worry about. It is not surprising, then, for mothers to wonder if they are perhaps wrong in feeling anxious and upset at hearing their child in distress.

Later on in the book the author alleviates any concern by stating that the baby will sort out and obliterate unpleasant moments anyway, so his crying doesn't really matter.[4] Granted, the healthy mind tends to remember the more pleasant aspects of life. However, the unpleasant happenings are still recorded, and are there to stay.[5]

Why do parents hesitate? If they have not read any of the numerous books on child rearing, then they have certainly leafed through a copy of Dr. Spock's *Baby and Child Care*. Among many middle class families in the United States, a well-used copy of this book has replaced the *Holy Bible* by the bedside. It has been translated into over twenty-nine languages, and over twenty-one million copies have been sold in the United States alone.[6]

"Better not let the child in your bed," he recommends. He reasons that when such a child has been picked up and treated to company for a number of nights, he learns to rouse himself from half awake to wide awake to have more fun.[7] But eating when one is hungry is fun too, yet it is also a very basic necessity. Wanting and needing to be near someone (and a baby's wants and needs are one and the same thing) is an equally important drive that needs to be fulfilled.

"Sometimes," Dr. Spock says elsewhere in his book, "the parents take a frightened child into bed with them so that they can all get some sleep." But this, he feels, can be a mistake because the child may "cling to the security of his parents' bed," even if his immediate anxiety decreases.[8] "So *always*," he concludes, "bring him promptly and firmly back to his own bed."

Who will speak for the child? "Why start something you cannot continue forever?" another doctor wrote to me. Forever? Yes, that would be a long time. But does it last "forever"? Of course not. Rest assured.

Parents should take pride in the fact that *they* are the ones the child seeks in time of need. To the child, they are more important than all the toys and teddy bears and dolls and blankets in the world. *Only they* can give him *true security.* How frightening that the child is discouraged from telling his parents that he would rather be with them than with his toys!

Once the young one has been subjected to automatic infant swingers, factory-produced glass bottles and rubber pacifiers, playpens, baby sitters, and day-care centers—when everything has been done to find substitutes for the parents—can't they, his parents, at least and at last take credit for being the ultimate form of security for their offspring and thus fulfill that part of their parenthood?

One sad story I heard concerned a couple who had followed the advice of never allowing their child into their bed. But since the child was so persistent in getting out of his own bed, they locked their bedroom door one night. The following morning they found him curled up and asleep against the outside of their bedroom door. The child had gotten as close to his parents as he could.

But today's ideal is to have a meticulous, pretty, attractive room for each child. A room with children's pictures on the wall, cuddly teddy bears that play little tunes, soft dolls that wind up and say "Hold me tight," numerous toys, and a little night light to keep the world from disappearing at night.

Pretty? Certainly! "But, Mommy, it is so *lonely!*"

Although he admits that his advice is not definitely harmless from a psychological point of view, Dr. Spock nevertheless relates his suggestion for handling the insistent toddler. When a climbing-out-of-bed problem in a two-year-old has gotten completely out of hand, he suggests that the parent rig a string netting over the top of the crib. He urges that it should never be spoken of as a punishment or a threat. The mother can refer to it cheerfully as a top on the bed to make a cozy house for the child to stay in and sleep in. She can even ask the child's help in tying it on.[9] No word is spoken, however, about what happens after the cheerfulness wears off and the real reason for his climbing out of bed arises again.

And all this misery simply because of that taboo: "Don't take your children into bed with you." Misery because we are urged to ignore a basic human need. We are bombarded by warnings that evil and terrible things are going to happen when we take the children in with us. The subject of sex is exposed. Consequences such as overdependence, homosexuality, and neurosis are mentioned. And whenever possible, samples are given of a Dr. so-and-so who knows of several neurotics (or homosexuals, or persons who are overly dependent) who, aha, slept with their parents or siblings until they were in their teens.

Recently an article on disturbed children appeared in a child psychiatry journal. It stated that over eleven percent of the children in a particular institute were recorded as sleeping with their parents. The article did not stress, however, that a significant majority of 89% did *not* sleep with their parents. At least their sleeping patterns were not coded. Should the connection between co-family sleeping and emotional problems indeed be so strong, then sleeping together within the family would, according to this study, hold a most favorable position.

Other negative advice urges parents to place their own comfort and importance first. Yet parents are willing to discard this advice once they have tried co-family sleeping, and have seen the results. What's more, once they have tried it, they don't *want* to change. Their children are happier, too.

One mother wrote that, before her first child was born, she read all the "right" books in order to prepare herself for rearing her children. "I had simply memorized 'a crib is for sleeping, and a playpen is for playing.' We thought that separate beds was the way to do it—society's demand that they would have to learn some time! We did not last very long though," this mother continued, "when we realized that we were developing clinging pre-schoolers during the day, especially during the morning rush."

Drugs are used to suppress lactation. Drugs are used to suppress fatigue. Drugs are used to suppress emotions. And drugs are used to cause sleepiness, even in children. Today, say Luce and Segal, there are over thirty million Americans who cope with anxiety, insomnia, tension, and emotional distress by taking drugs—often without close contact with their doctors. There seems to be a strong and most dangerous sleep myth that insomnia can be cured by simply swallowing a pill.[10] This popular, uneducated conception has persuaded many, incorrectly, that sleep is purchasable at any price. Many actually believe that a pill will cure rather than mask the underlying cause of sleeplessness. Some parents insist on sedatives for their child when he does not fall asleep at pre-determined schedules.[11]

I am greatly disturbed by the fact that a twentieth-century doctor would advise the use of drugs to induce sleep in an apparently normal child who is having difficulty falling asleep. It is most alarming that these dangerous drugs are given to children, when love, compassion, companionship, and understanding would have solved the problem, assuming that the sleep problem has not been caused by allergies: sugar, milk, to name a few. Nevertheless, one doctor advises in his book on child care that if the firm approach mixed with a dose of compassion is not successful, the parent may ask the doctor for medication. There is nothing wrong with doing this, he feels.[12] And thus we begin early teaching that life's problems can be solved with a pill. How far-removed have we become from clean, fresh, healthy, happy living?

Everything possible is suggested to the parents to prevent the child from entering the parental bed and to keep him in his own; even to the point of drugging him into a state of unconsciousness which is supposed to be a good night's sleep. And so, "good" reasons are found to justify separate sleeping.

- I need my sleep.
- We all sleep better when the children sleep in their own beds.
- I am more comfortable sleeping alone.
- Husband is against it.
- Bed is too small.
- Room is too small for a larger bed.
- Because custom indicates it should be this way and gives no alternative.
- Complete ignorance.
- Baby is too active physically.
- Books.
- Relatives say, "You'll be sorry!"
- Pediatrician's advice that baby should not come between parents, in bed or otherwise.
- Mother is too active in sleep, awakens children and husband.
- Baby makes too many noises.
- Afraid that we will roll on baby.

- Interferes with sex.
- He should learn to become self-reliant.
- He should learn to depend on God's love to protect him and help him with his fears.
- Doctor said that breastfeeding him in bed results in ear infections.

In the *Childbirth Education Association News Letter* of Greater Minneapolis-St. Paul, Minnesota (August 1973), an article by Dr. William G. Crook reported on the increase of ear infections in babies over the past twenty years. "Formula allergy was first blamed," he states. "But recent research suggests that the blame be put on the fact that babies get fluid in their ears because many of them take their bottle lying down."[13] Further research indicates, however, that cow's milk may, indeed, be the culprit.

The article further comments on the "frequently made observation that ear trouble is uncommon in breastfed babies." Whether he is being nursed in a chair or in bed, the breastfeeding baby is frequently lying in a horizontal position, and on his side. Breastfeeding mothers need not fear, then, that their baby will necessarily get an ear infection when being nursed in bed.

Another concern of parents was the supposed connection between caries in a child's teeth and night nursing. The following question was posed by the mother of a nursing two-year-old.

> *Help!* I have a two-year-old who wakes several times during the night. This has not bothered me, nor has his sleeping with us. But now he has eight cavities. I've been told by a number of dentists that this is due largely to night nursing. Those who have not actually suggested I stop nursing have told me I must face the problem of future cavities in great number. Obviously dental work at this age will be traumatic, but so will stopping the night nursing. What do I do?

If caries are due largely to night nursing, then the mouths of children throughout the world—and throughout history—must have been in a frightfully deteriorated state. In the La Leche League publication *New Beginnings* (May-June 1986, pg. 59), an article on tooth decay and the older nursing child states that, even though some dentists have recommended to their breastfeeding mothers that night nursing could cause tooth decay, these recommendations are not supported by current scientific literature. "There have been no systematic studies that link extended or night nursing to tooth decay of any kind." Some researchers even feel that "the active anti-infective properties of human milk may actually help prevent cavities by inhibiting the growth of bacteria in the mouth." By now it is fairly well-established that the state of our teeth is largely due to the kind of food we eat daily over a number of months and years. This implies the child as well as the mother. Indeed there have been breastfed children who, sometimes within a very short time, developed a number of cavities. Night nursing, not being the norm in our society, is easily blamed as the culprit. Night nursing is *not* the reason. La Leche League has been gathering data (thus far inconclusive) as to the causes of caries in young breastfed children. Suggestions as to the causes range from the dietary habits of the child to the mother's state of health before and during pregnancy, hereditary implications, and medications such as prophylactic antibiotics in liquid form given to the child. Much research needs to be done. In the meantime, eat wholesome foods, fresh fruits and vegetables, stay away from sugar and other refined foods, and nurse your toddler at night as well as during the day with no worry. Surely nature would not be so cruel as to inflict upon young innocent children the agony of cavities as a result of their seeking comfort, security, love, and nourishment from their mother. Rest assured. Nurse your toddler at night as well as during the day, as nature had intended. The answer to the question of caries lies elsewhere.

A matter of deep concern to new parents considering taking their children into bed with them is Sudden Infant Death, also known as "crib death," "overlying," or "cot death." Sudden Infant Death has been with us since ancient times. It is even mentioned in the Bible.

> Then came there two women, that were harlots, unto the king, and stood before him. And the one woman said, O my Lord, I and this woman dwell in one house; and I was delivered of a child with her in the house. And it came to pass the third day after that I was delivered that this woman was delivered also; and we were together; there was no stranger with us in the house, save we two in the house. And this woman's child died in the night because she overlaid it (1st Kings 3: 16 AV).

That these tragedies are necessarily caused by "overlying," however, has been declared erroneous.

As many societies still practice today, mothers routinely used to sleep with their infants. When a mother awakened to find her child dead, she assumed she must have rolled on top of him and caused his death.[14] But one author suggests that if indeed the death was caused by "overlying," the mother or wet nurse may well have been drugged or intoxicated.[15]

According to the National Foundation for Sudden Infant Deaths, SIDS (Sudden Infant Death Syndrome) causes from 7,000 to 8,000 infant deaths annually in the United States.[16] Another source claims that this number may be as high as 25,000.

An apparently healthy baby, usually between the ages of three weeks and seven months, is put to bed without the slightest hint that things are out of the ordinary. Some time later he is found dead without any demonstrable disease. Often there is no evidence of a struggle, nor has anyone heard the baby struggling.

SIDS occurs during naptime or during the night. Many theories as to the cause of SIDS have been put forth. However, none of these has been definitely proven and most have been discounted. According to the National Sudden Infant Death Syndrome Foundation, "deaths are often erroneously attributed to smothering, but to date—1986—no common cause or method of prevention has been determined." (Encyclopedia of Associations. 20th edition. Vol 1, 1986. Gale Research Comp., Detroit, Michigan). Furthermore, one must question the logistics of this tragedy: How can overlying occur in a crib or cot? Did the mother or "overlyer" crawl into the crib with the baby?

The foundation further believes that there has not been an increase in the number of SIDS cases in recent years. One simply hears more about them because there is currently more extensive publicity about them than in the past. Studies conducted by the foundation in many areas of the world consistently show figures of two to three SIDS deaths per 1,000 live births. Many communities now report the cause of death as Sudden Infant Death, or "crib death." Unfortunately, other areas still list them as suffocation or overlying which, the NFSID states, is a tragedy since it implies neglect or carelessness on the part of the family.

One such newspaper article urges all doctors to routinely caution parents against the "dangerous" practice of sleeping in the same bed with an infant. The article continues with the report of a study of 336 crib deaths in Shelba County, Tennessee. According to an investigator,

24 cases (7%) were almost certainly due to overlying and, in another 49 cases (14%), this was a very strong possibility. The investigators admitted that they *were not sure*, however.

When this article was brought to the attention of the La Leche League International Board of Directors, which suggests taking a nursing infant to bed, Mary White, a member of the executive board, replied that this study was out of date, and had been disproven by later studies. Such accounts border on irresponsible scare stories.

The National Foundation for Sudden Infant Deaths stresses the important fact that Sudden Infant Deaths cannot be predicted. There is no known way to definitely prevent their occurrence.[18] Even so, according to an article in a 1971 *La Leche League News*, breastfed babies are rarely victims of the sudden-death syndrome[19]. We may also consider the probability that the greater majority of babies do not sleep with their mothers. It is significant to realize, then, that in spite of separate sleeping, it is nowhere mentioned that the rate of SIDS has dropped from a hundred years ago, when most babies did sleep with their mothers. Nor is the occurrence of Sudden Infant Death Syndrome higher in societies in which Mother and Baby routinely sleep together.

In a letter to the American Medical News (Febr. 13, 1981), a doctor from India commented that all nine of his siblings were born at home, and nursed and slept with his mother as babies. Cribs did not exist. *"Take away the crib and you will prevent crib death."*

If we consider the infant himself, we see that nature has given him very strong means of survival. In some ways he is tremendously strong, his reflexes are superb, and he has a good voice. When he lies on his stomach, he has a set of reflexes that make it almost impossible for him to smother in that position. When the free flow of air is threatened, he raises his head off the bed, and turns it from one side to the other. He begins to crawl with his legs, and can even lift himself up on his arms.[20] When lying on his side or back, Baby's arms are almost continuously flexed so that his hands are close to his face, ready to push away things that threaten him. As any mother can testify, it is frequently difficult to straighten a baby's arms when putting a little shirt on him.

Additionally, the NFSID reports that even when infants are covered by bedding, the amount of oxygen is not reduced to the point of suffocation.[21] If the child finds himself in an uncomfortable or alarming position, he will certainly do everything possible to communicate this to the parent by crying and kicking. Sudden Infant Deaths happen more frequently with little boys between the ages of two and six months. At this time they are stronger than the newborn, yet more susceptible to the tragedy.

A mother of eight children wrote: "One night I could not sleep and decided to observe Baby. The infant was three weeks old, and sleeping between my husband and me. Baby was lying on her back: arms bent, fists close to her face. Father was sleeping too, but started to roll over onto the child. The infant immediately put out her arms and feet and began to whimper. In his sleep my husband reacted to the touch and sound and moved away from the child.

"I began to nurse her, and became interested in seeing what would happen if I changed my position so that my breast fully covered her face, thereby inhibiting breathing. I changed my position and, after what seemed minutes, the baby suddenly jerked her head away from the breast, gasped several times, and was fine again. She then resumed nursing."

Another mother told me what happened when she moved too close to her tiny two-and-a-half-week-old son. She said that the baby protested so vigorously that no one could have possibly slept through it. This mother and her husband, whose friends had lost a baby in crib death, found they slept much better knowing that their baby was with them.

There seems to be every indication that Sudden Infant Deaths are caused by mysterious internal causes rather than external ones. However, if the fear of possibly harming the new infant creates such mental anguish that neither the mother nor father can sleep well, putting Baby in a cradle right next to Mother is a much better solution. The mother can still feel that she is right there when her baby needs her, and she will not have to get out of bed to nurse her infant. If she is bottlefeeding, she can get the bottle, and then snuggle up in bed with her baby while she gives him his milk. After Baby is put back in his little bed, Mother will be able to rub Baby's back and gently rock the cradle while resting. She will still feel the closeness of her precious new one, which is indeed a wonderful feeling. Once the child is a few months old, he can be taken into the parental bed.

From the beginning of time until quite recently, most infants slept with their mother or mother substitute. In many parts of the world this practice is still the norm. In the last one hundred years or so, however, it has been the custom of the Western world to have Baby sleep by himself. But according to research, there has been no drop in incidents of Sudden Unexplained Infant Deaths.

And so, as La Leche League's manual, *The Womanly Art of Breastfeeding,* says: "When your baby wakes at night, you need only tuck him into bed with you, start nursing him, and the two of you can drop off to sleep together. It's quite safe—we've all done it, and Baby loves the warm closeness which usually helps him drop off to sleep sooner than he might do otherwise."[22]

4

The Importance of
Sleeping Together

You have touched me. I have grown.

A Kikiyu chief of East Africa once spoke these words: "At night when there was no sun to warm me, my mother's arms, her body took its place..."[1] What a truly beautiful feeling is experienced by both Mother and Child when they sleep together.

Love is exchanged between people, not between people and things. Love is a two-way street in which a person not only gives love but also needs to receive it.[2] In order for a person to be able to give and receive love freely as an adult, it is necessary that he was able to give and receive love freely when he was a child.[3] Even the infant, says Montagu, is born not only wanting and needing to be loved, but also wanting and needing to love others. He should not have to transfer his giving to an inanimate object, because this thing does not give love in return.[4] And all evidence indicates, according to Salk and Kramer, that the newborn infant also has an impressive capacity to observe the world through his senses.[5] For too long it was erroneously believed that babies are rather dull and selfish creatures, only wanting and taking when they have the notion. This belief, says Montagu, has done a great deal of damage to human beings and to society.

A baby or young child who is strongly urged to fall asleep by himself and stay in his own bed at all times is forced, when the need arises, to "mother" himself at night. A thumb, bottle, blanket, or teddy bear takes the place of another person, of love. He may suppress his need for his parents at that time, and convince himself that he does not need them. Unfortunately, a suppressed need is not erased, although it may lie dormant within the person for many, many years.

"It seems to be the law of nature," writes Ratner, "that human beings need a certain total amount of time and devotion from their mothers. If the mother does not give of herself to her child when the child is most dependent—a force which liberates the child to become independent by the security obtained—nature has a peculiar way of exacting compensation later in the child's history."[6]

In our society today we give no second thought to a young child frantically clutching his blanket. We unquestioningly accept advice that urges the separation of mother and child. Babies are either left to cry or given an article serving as a mother substitute. Questioning a possible correlation, Dr. Salk noted that more than half the hospital beds are filled with mental patients.[7] Many adults are still struggling with unmet infantile needs of their own.[8] Many mothers and fathers have been left with frustration that results from an unfulfilled need, the need to be "the sun," to be the all-goodness, giving source to the baby.

Mothers have told me that, as much as they loved and cared for their children who were bottlefed and slept in their own cribs, there was frequently a feeling of, "Shouldn't I do something more for them?" as they kissed their children good night. They did not experience this feeling with their breastfed children, especially if they all slept together. Instead, they felt total fulfillment.

True love should be free to be exchanged at any time, unconditionally, whether day or night. It is this freedom, the knowledge that there are no set times, that makes it beautiful and important.

The mother who takes her child into her arms and comforts him at night, and then peacefully falls asleep with her little one touching her body, knows and feels deep down that she is not only giving but also receiving something that words can't describe. She feels that she is part of the universe, a link in the chain of life. She forms a momentary oneness with her child which, as the need diminishes, will flower into a twosome again, much like the flowering at birth. A glow fills her body, and this glow radiates to her other children and her husband. But this feeling of total fulfillment can only exist when there is no frustration or restraint.

In her keynote address during La Leche League's Fourth Convention, Marian Tompson, President, said, "I think we have much yet to learn about the special relationship among Mother, Father and Child. I strongly suspect that loving parents protect the vulnerable infant from psychological and spiritual assaults, as well as the more apparent and accepted ones, in ways not yet understood. There is more there than the eye can see, or the mind understand, at this point. It can be felt, especially by the breastfeeding mother in her oneness with her baby."

According to Montagu, it does make some difference in the developing personality of the child whether he is breastfed and whether he is permitted to sleep in the same room or bed with his parents or siblings. With such experiences, the child becomes more demonstrative in showing affection, says Montagu, and seems better equipped to deal competently with social processes. Parents have verified that such a child also seems to have a higher degree of empathy for other members in the family. This can only graduate to a feeling of empathy for others outside the family unit, a compassion that would be helpful to others in withstanding the impersonal pressures of our times.[9]

The ability to show such affection and understanding of others arises from the satisfaction of self-esteem, which depends primarily upon a dependent relationship with the parents, and which necessitates during the first few years in the child's life the almost constant presence of other persons, preferably his mother, his father and his siblings.[10] La Leche League reports that studies show a direct relationship between the amount of mothering a baby gets and his physical and intellectual development.[11] Has it not been said that loving a baby is a lot like nurturing a plant? The more care it is given, the more fruit it bears.

The experience of sharing the same bed or bedroom results in a feeling of togetherness, of unity, of belonging.[12] It spreads love. A feeling of, "I'm part of this family. I belong to you, to all of mankind," is perceived even while asleep.

Sleeping together has a soothing effect on misunderstandings and harsh words spoken during the day. For an average of eight hours, in the stillness of the night, and the relaxing and disarming state of sleep, those who sleep together touch as if to say, "You are all right. I'm all right. We remain in touch with one another."[13] It is such a wonderful feeling to wake up in the middle of the night, and to kiss a loved one while he or she is asleep.

Montagu writes that physical contact "appears to act as a principle regulator of broodiness,"[14] which may be freely translated as meaning "mothering" or "parenting" (since men, too, may exhibit a certain amount of this behavior). Physical contact fulfills desires of that special feeling of parenthood, giving satisfaction to the protective instinct called mother-love, or parent-love.

Might this be one reason why, once a woman has successfully nursed an infant, it is rare that she will want to bottlefeed again? And does it explain why parents, once they have had their children sleep with them, rarely reverse their decisions? Or why a new mother so instinctively treasures the contact with her newborn infant?

Unfortunately, our society is not a society of touch. Even some breastfed babies, because of the mother's fear of criticism of "indecent" exposure, touch little of their mother's skin other than the nipple and areola. Sleeping in the nude, or with a brief nightgown, compensates for some of this. The baby will lovingly caress and touch his mother, or manipulate or hold the other nipple while nursing. This seems to be a universal trait of the nursing child. I have observed such nipple-holding in various photographs of nursing children in other countries.[15] And a number of American friends have noticed this action in their own babies.

If we accept the importance of continued cutaneous stimulation between child and parent,* then it becomes obvious that this exchange should not only take place between Mother and Child, but also between Father and Child. But in civilized countries such as ours, men are more fully clothed than women, and the actual chance of skin-to-skin contact is practically nullified. Add to this the fact that most fathers are gone during the greater portion of the child's waking hours, and it becomes clear that sleeping together would add considerably to the cutaneous interchange between father and child. One mother wrote that her husband frequently slept with their baby on his chest.

Working mothers I have talked with have further suggested that sleeping with their baby and encouraging night nursings increased their mother-baby contact. Aside from the obvious benefits to the baby, it also helped to ease the mother's deep concern about her absence. However, this tactile demonstration of affection between parents and their children, especially with children of the opposite sex, is frequently open to misunderstanding and ridicule.[16] It is frowned upon because touching in our culture is to a large extent associated with sex, and the great importance of the emotional transaction that takes place through the skin, by touching, has until quite recently been ignored. "This stress on the sexual element in all forms of intimate behavior," writes Morris in *Intimate Behavior,* "has resulted in a massive

*See *Touching: The Human Significance of the Skin* by Ashley Montagu.

inhibition of our non-sexual body intimacies. When these intimacies apply to parents and offspring, then Beware, Oedipus!; to siblings, Beware, incest!; to close same-sex friends, Beware, homosexuality!; to close opposite-sex friends, Beware, adultery!; and to many casual friends, Beware, promiscuity!"

According to Montagu, it is only since the 1940's that knowledge of both the physical and emotional functions of the skin has been acquired and recorded.[17] But, as is frequent with scientific data, the initial research is far ahead of general interest or acceptance.

In an article, "I'm Joe's Skin," published by *Reader's Digest* in 1972, many of the technical and physical aspects of the skin are mentioned, such as the complexity of the nervous system, the intricacy of the network of blood vessels.[18] But the emotional function of the skin, the subject to which Dr. Montagu dedicated an entire book, *Touching: The Human Significance of the Skin,* is not once brought to the reader's attention. Dr. Montagu continually stresses the importance of touching the young child. In order to be tender, loving and caring, to be considerate and understanding, to be able to freely give oneself to the needs of his offspring, one must have been shown consideration, understanding, and must have had all his needs fulfilled by a loving parent in his own early years, indeed from the moment of birth.[19]

When joy and comfort are unconditionally experienced in the arms of his mother, or the proximity of other persons, the child learns to associate these feelings with people, and learns that he can turn to his fellow human beings in time of need. It makes him feel good about himself. He is worth attention. Realization of high self-worth leads to high self-esteem.

Today it is "the thing" for adults or older adolescents who cannot relate to others to try group therapy. Sensitivity or encounter groups have become popular from coast to coast. In some groups of sensitivity training, members are not allowed to talk with or even look at each other, but must communicate through touch." One is encouraged to embrace others, caress them, hold hands with them, bathe in the nude with them, and be massaged by them.

This is very, very difficult for most American adults. "One reason," says James Kenny, co-author of an article that appeared in *Marriage,* 1971, "is that our physical isolation from one another has been plotted since infancy. Single beds. Separate rooms. Stop fighting. Don't touch."[20]

The importance of co-family sleeping is further emphasized by its role in the transition period of an infant's total dependency on his mother (pre-birth) and his physiological independence of her, usually by the age of three years or older. This is an aspect of child rearing that is, however, seldom considered in our Western culture. "Indeed," writes Newton, "it may last less than one minute—until the cord is cut before the delivery of the placenta."[21] And the infant, given his first bottle, has become independent of her. Anyone can now mother him.

This transition phase is repeatedly present in those societies that seem to produce emotionally-stable people. According to Newton, the fact that the components of this phase (namely close mother-baby contact, sensitivities to crying, child spacing, and prolonged breastfeeding) occur again and again in many of the primitive* and traditional cultures suggests that there may be a strong mechanism involved in this interrelation of patterning.[22] It is important, therefore, to recognize and compare the effect that the presence or absence of the transition phase has upon the people involved.

In primitive societies, and others not influenced by western culture, unrestricted breastfeeding (therefore also night nursing) is nearly always present. Newton cites several sample cases in which breastfeeding takes precedence over any other activity in which the mother may be engaged, such as selling her vegetables in the market, although she may be extremely anxious to make the sale. Children are nursed freely, and frequently sleep with the nipple of the mother's breast in their mouths at night. The weaning process is slow and doesn't usually occur before the age of two. Every attempt is nearly always made to soothe a crying child.[23]

People who emphasize the transition phase tend to feel strongly about the spacing of children. This spacing will insure the full energy and attention of the mother toward her youngest child. Although frequent day and night nursing will, in most cases, lead to an absence of ovulation for at least seven months (and frequently up to eighteen, twenty-four, or more months postpartum), the concern of another pregnancy before the baby has reached a certain independent stage is so strong that many customs keep a taboo upon intercourse until the child has reached this stage of development.[24]

*Primitive people is used in its anthropological sense, meaning people who are without written language.

The transition phase shows considerable variation among individual people and societies. But, as mentioned above, the fact that it occurs among most societies that tend to produce stable individuals is an extremely important factor to consider.

Running counter to the fulfillment of the transition phase and the need for bodily contact, however, is the modern trend toward minimum touching, early weaning, letting baby cry, and isolated sleeping (away from any other human being). According to Newton, the muting of the transition phase is one of the most striking differences between the primitive, traditional cultures and our own industrial culture.[25]

From the moment a healthy child is born, he is placed in a warmer, then a bassinet, then a crib with a bottle, and encouraged to be by himself. This custom is so strong that many a mother worries tremendously when her baby seems to need to be held "so much," and when he does not seem to want to sleep by himself. The parent spends hours awake at night because Baby cannot be put down in his bassinet without beginning to cry, and she is quite concerned when, at three months, the infant is still not sleeping through the night by himself. The "good" baby sleeps through the night. The "not-so-good" baby doesn't. It seems to be a status symbol, a sign of good mothering, when one's baby sleeps at night. "Does your infant sleep through the night yet?" is a question of great importance to some people, including doctors. "Is he happy?" is often an afterthought, or not asked at all.

Mothers who have their children sleep with them, however, are rarely concerned about nighttime waking. But aside from social pressures, it is no wonder that the mother who has to get out of her nice warm bed should be so anxious for her child to sleep through the night.

"Why doesn't my child sleep through the night?" We hear this complaint from many mothers. Yet I believe there are quite a few adults who can attest to waking up once or twice during the night, even if it is ever so slightly. When a child awakens, perhaps as he turns over, he finds himself alone. This doesn't make the little ones happy. The child thus seeks his parents. Similarly, when he spends time alone with his toys during the day, he will come running into the kitchen after a while for a hug or kiss or just to say hello. Even little babies, like adults, awake slightly during their sleep. They will look around for a few seconds, and go back to sleep, if they are content.

I overheard one mother tell another mother: "You know, my baby definitely sleeps longer when she sleeps next to me. Time and again I would be resting with her when she took her nap. Several times during her sleep she would open her eyes, look right at me, turn around, and go back to sleep. When she has slept by herself, she would awaken and start crying when she did not see me. And that was usually the end of her nap." The other mother replied enthusiastically that her baby did exactly the same thing.

Bad dreams and nightmares are frightening experiences. Some children (and adults, too) are bothered by them more than others. And even though we are repeatedly told that this is not really abnormal, one wonders if this unpleasant experience is normal. "Bad dreams and other night disturbances in sleep are frequently related to the child's fear of being deserted by his parents," says Montagu.[26]

When a child sleeps with his parents, a sense of security is transmitted from the parents to the child. Likewise, children sleeping together transmit a certain sense of security. Parents of large families, who have reared children both in the conventional way and in allowing them in their bed, feel that sleeping together has definitely reduced the occurrence of bad dreams almost to the vanishing point. They have realized that co-family sleeping is a preventive measure, rather than a means of soothing the child *after* he has already had his bad dream.

One mother wrote, "My son says he feels better if he is near me and can touch me when he has a bad dream which, since he has been sleeping with us regularly, is very infrequent."

Luce and Segal seem to feel that the occurrence of nightmares is dependent upon dream patterns. During a nightmare they report that children may, in their deep delta sleep, scream and howl. They will fight off invisible monsters, shrieking for help and continuing to cry for their mother even when being held by the parent. It is difficult to awaken the child from these terrifying dreams. He rarely remembers them.[27]

Luce and Segal also feel that the occurrence of nightmares is rather normal. Parent's experiences seem to indicate that the child who sleeps by himself has more nightmares than the child who sleeps in the secure presence of another person. Nightmares may be "normal" in the sense that they appear with relative frequency in our Western culture. Are they, however, normal in the sense of the process of human development?

Perhaps more research needs to be done on sleep patterns of the child who sleeps alone with a bottle, the child who sleeps alone but is breastfed on demand, and the child who sleeps in bed with someone. Many parents feel that no research is necessary. The evidence is there.

The fear of being alone in a situation that is potentially frightening or dangerous is real in most people. Darkness increases fear. Even in a situation that should not be frightening, such as sleeping in one's own bed, the imagination of both children and adults alike can play unpleasant tricks. Thus, sleeping alone, even though one may get used to it, may not feel quite as safe as sleeping with someone else. The sense of "He'll protect me. He'll help me. He'll hear it before I will" provides a sense of protection and safety and comfort. Many mothers have related the sense of fear they experience when their husbands are out of town for a few nights. As one cartoon put it: it is not the dark I'm afraid of, it's the things I can't see in it.

Fear of being alone may cause insomnia, or difficulty in falling asleep and remaining asleep. In Bowlby's book, *Separation,* much reference is made to the reassuring effect the presence of a companion has on a person when he is in the dark or in a dangerous situation.[28] It is especially present in young children. The immediate reaction of a person who experiences fear is to seek out another person and stay with that person for a considerable length of time after the fear has passed.[29] But most of us, in due time, learn to conquer fear of the unknown to a reasonable degree. Eventually, we learn to sleep alone quite peacefully. We also learn to go to school by ourselves, and to handle stress. Some people learn more quickly than others. But everyone benefits from gentle understanding and acceptance when he is confronted by fear.

Sleep was once considered to be a state of dullness, of deadness that was something unavoidable and necessary, but nonetheless rather wasted as far as any usefulness with respect to learning and experiencing was concerned. Indeed, many a poet has likened sleep to death by referring to it as "eternal sleep."

> Downy sleep
> Death's counterfeit
>
> Shakespeare

Until recently, say Luce and Segal, anthropologists didn't pay much attention to sleeping behavior as they studied the living habits of other people. At night everyone simply went to sleep, and studies were resumed the following day. Nor do child therapists usually bother to obtain information concerning the patient's sleeping history, even though valuable information could be revealed by doing so.[30]

That the mind is not inactive but is able to perceive while asleep has been proven by the fact that a person can learn while sleeping. The science of *Hypnopaedia,* or learning while asleep, is part of the repertoire of scientific literature. During the 1950's, when sleep re-searchers began to demonstrate that human sleep follows a rhythmic pattern varying from light to very deep sleep, they banished forever the common notion that one part of the night is just like any other.[31]

One does not simply "go to sleep and wake up" in the morning. Even deep sleep is unlike a coma. Laboratory studies have shown that it is possible to listen during sleep, and to discriminate among sounds. Children and babies may not consciously remember what goes on during their sleep, but, according to Luce and Segal, we no longer assume that they were untouched by the fights and commotions that went on during their sleep. So, too, a warm, loving atmosphere has an important effect on them.

Much still needs to be learned about sleep, for it is an integral part of life's rhythm and relevant to every aspect of it. But children do not wait for scientific discoveries. Their needs are *now.* Ten years from now will be too late. And what simpler task is there than to give our time, love, and security to our children while we are asleep!

"It should be emphasized," said Edwina Froehlich, one of La Leche League's founding mothers, "that the willingness to accept the idiosyn-crasies of parenthood, which are very different from the state of childlessness, are the first real signs that the person is ready to accept the obligations of parenthood."[32]

Many parents have rather unbending ideas about what a small child should be like, what he should have, and when he should have it. "Most parents will not admit," says Chisolm, "that these are really only matters of convenience for themselves or for the local custom, and that they have no real universal validity."[33]

Society has taken away a baby's right to be dependent on his mother. Left to sleep by himself, states Salk, he often engages in self-mothering, in self-stimulation such as rocking back and forth, head-banging, thumb-sucking, fingering his ears, nose, or hair.[34] He may even make a "nipple" out of a corner of a blanket to suck on.

Among the non-literate people who generally give their children all the tactile stimulation they require, these forms of self-manipulation seldom occur.[35] Yet some authors feel that it is the "right" of every human infant to have his own bed and bedroom.[36] They try to convince parents of this. The needs of the person in question, the young child, are never considered. And to whom else can a statement like this be directed than to those few who can afford to give each child his own bedroom? As society becomes wealthier, human interaction seems to become more poor.

We all have a need to be understood by others, intellectually, physically, as well as emotionally, and it is no less strong in the first few years of life. As adults, we may tend to suppress certain needs at certain times. However, a child has not yet learned to do this. He will usually attempt to communicate his needs. Nor can a child wait very long for a need fulfillment. *A young child has an inborn safety valve which, if allowed to sound off naturally and freely, will announce when he can no longer remain in one particular state; that unless he gets relief, he will be carrying a burden which is heavier than is good for him. If he gets too cold, too hungry, too warm, too lonely, too frightened, the child will give indication that he needs a change, that he needs relief from the situation in which he finds himself. And the need for relief is now, not later.*

A child seeking the security of his parents' bed at night is indicating that he needs a change from a situation that upset him—cold, loneliness, fright, dreams. The child who sleeps with his parents needs only to move a little closer to his mother or father.

How do children learn to love? How do children learn to wait? Child psychologists' records of observations indicate that it is the baby who is immediately and unconditionally loved, immediately and unconditionally waited on, who learns to love and to wait. Indulgence in this respect at an early age results in patience as an adult. The person who is *not* frustrated in his early years is more capable of enduring frustration as an adult.[37]

We all feel overcrowded from time to time, and the idea of "peace and quiet" can become very attractive. But human beings are social creatures who need one another, and for most of us a short time of solitude is sufficient.[38]

A young child has even less of a need for being alone; as a matter of fact, he usually does not *want* to be alone for very long. And when he does, it should be of his own choice, not ours. The young child doesn't expect giving and receiving love to stop at nighttime, with lights out, and be resumed the following morning. It shouldn't be this way.

When the child of a very large, middle-class family saw that a neighborhood friend from a family of two had his own bedroom, he asked his mother if his friend was being punished by having to sleep all by himself. It is lonesome to be alone, and most of us don't like it. It is wonderful to be close to those we love, and most of us thrive on it. The importance of co-family sleeping arrangements, be they parents and child, or child and child, lies in the fact that people thrive on literally being in touch with one another, even while asleep.

5

Need vs. Habit

It is the law of human life, as certain as gravity; to live fully, we must learn to use things and love people . . . not love things and use people.

Maria Montessori

"It is not in the nature of nature," writes Salk, "to provide organisms with biological tendencies unless such tendencies have survival value."[1] It would be wise to listen to nature instead of trying to suppress or ignore it. Certain aspects of human life are not matters of opinion, but are determined biologically. The need of a child to sleep with members of his family is not a subject to be determined by our opinion. It should be determined by his emotional wants.

The wants of a well-adjusted human being are his needs. It is when his needs are not fulfilled that his wants become excessive in an attempt to fulfill suppressed needs.

We are born needing. We need air, food, sleep, and shelter. We need intellectual and physical stimulation. We need to be loved and touched.[2] If any of these needs goes fully or even partially unattended, the person hurts; and in the case of an emotional wound, the person may spend the rest of his life struggling to soothe the initial hurt.[3]

Gesell feels that a child passes through predictable stages of development at predictable times.[4] Thus, what might seem to become a habit may simply be a gratification of a need.

In his book *Child Under Six*, Hymes describes a habit as an action that can easily be broken. "If you run into any major difficulty at all," he writes, "*Beware!* You are probably not dealing with an old outworn habit. The chances are that you are tampering with a human need."[5]

If the body indicates a need for food, treating it like a habit and disregarding it will not make the hunger go away. Ignoring the sensation of wanting to lie down and sleep will not forever cure one from having to sleep eight hours a day. The child who seeks his parents' bed at night is also expressing a basic need. And this need must be satisfied at its own time and pace.

The child who is allowed to be with his parents will gradually mature to the point of being satisfied with sleeping elsewhere, usually seeking the companionship of another member of the family. If the child *wants* to sleep with his parents, then he *needs* to. If he crawls into his parents' bed but is then content to be taken to a sibling's bed, it obviously doesn't matter to him where he sleeps as long as he feels secure. This has now been extended to include sleeping with his siblings, a pet, or perhaps even by himself.

For some strange reason we tend to think that to satisfy a child's need is to make it into an unbreakable habit, when in truth the exact opposite is true.[6] When our children develop a "good" habit, or one that suits us, we are afraid it is not going to last. But when our children develop a "bad" habit, or one that does not suit us, we are afraid it is going to last forever. So many people are afraid that their children will not grow up. We are told to feed a baby solids with a spoon at three weeks of age, lest he never learn to eat solids, let alone with a spoon. We are told to toilet train them at the age of one or they will never stop wearing diapers. We should begin to discipline them at one month; otherwise, they will never listen to us. Children must always sleep in their own beds or they will always want to sleep with their parents. It is commonly believed that babies need to be weaned by the mother. And yet when weaning is left totally up to the child, it happens in a natural, healthy, relaxed way, usually between the ages of one and four years. When the child no longer needs the direct physical contact with his mother, then he weans himself from the breast. Likewise, parents' experiences indicate that the healthy child will, in time, wean himself from the parental bed. Provided that the home environment is healthy, children will mature. As each need is fulfilled at each stage, they will move on and become more mature. (We did!)

It all goes back to listening to the child and trusting him. If a three-year-old told you, "I love you," would you believe him? Of course you would. Then why not believe him when he tells you that he is lonely or frightened, or not hungry or not sleepy? And if you suspect that this is not the real truth, you'd better look for an underlying reason that has difficulty coming out. Once you've decided to trust your child, it is amazing what a load it will take off your back. You can start communicating with him and allow him to *tell* you his feelings so you won't have to figure them out. You will build a trust that is magnificent and beautiful, leading to a lifetime of closeness. When you work in harmony with nature, things have a much better chance of going right, whether we're talking about growing vegetables, the healing arts, or rearing children. Just as there are seasons in nature, so it is in the lives of humankind. Trust that in sound surroundings your child will graduate from one state of development to the next. Just ask a grandparent, who has been through it all and has seen the changes. Such a person knows that nothing is constant but change itself.

I remember carrying my first infant throughout the day. Then she began to crawl and I no longer needed to hold her as frequently. I remember nursing her fifteen times a day. Now she is weaned and eats and drinks what we eat and drink. I used to take her with me wherever I went. And if I could not take her I stayed home. (Except if she was asleep.) She was happiest with this arrangement. Then, when she was about three years old, she took another step toward independence; she began to look forward to the occasional babysitter to read her a bedtime story and put her to bed.

A child who has his needs fulfilled will become an independent, secure person. But independence cannot be forced upon someone.[7] It takes time and growing at the individual's own pace. The more secure he is in the knowledge that he can always come back to his parents, the more independent he will become. We will only create problems if we regard his needing us at night as a problem that should be "cured."

Our Western society is so complex. Our very homes are far too complicated to let the child have the freedom of his domain. It is truly amazing how many restrictions we must place on him in his everyday life. The stove is dangerous, the electrical appliances are dangerous, "don't cross the street." It is a real eye opener to count the number of times we say "No!" or remind a child that he is dealing with potential danger. Should we, therefore, frustrate him even more by putting restrictions on emotional wants and needs?

The child's sleeping in the parental bed should not be regarded as a privilege, nor restricted for the fear of its becoming a habit. Rather, it should be understood as an important fulfillment of a basic human need. No matter where the child finds himself, whether as a single child or one of many siblings, whether living at the present time or a thousand years ago, whether living in the United States, in China, or somewhere deep in the jungle of Africa, his basic need for love and security has not and will not change, in spite of what social trends want us to believe.

6

Brief History of Childhood and Family Sleeping

Learning is ever in the freshness of its youth, even for the old.

Aeschylus

"It is rather unimaginable," writes Luce, "that separate sleeping arrangements and bedtime problems with children are as old as mankind, and indeed they are not. They are products of our modern civilization."[1]

How is it, then, that we have chapter upon chapter, discussion upon discussion, concerning a function that man has always performed, and which is so natural? How have we come to the present situation?

Our subject, of course, is the child, and as we briefly scan the history of the child, we see that he has not always had the place in the family that he has now. He has risen from being simply an offspring who needs to outgrow his younger years before reaching the level of a producing adult to the present when quite a fuss is being made over him. He has moved from sleeping securely and snugly next to his family members, to sleeping alone with only a teddy bear.

Turning the pages of history back to medieval times, it may be observed by the viewer of the arts that, until about the twelfth century, children were rarely depicted as children. Rather, they appeared as little adults, even to the extent of giving the naked body of a child (in the very few cases when it was exposed) the musculature of an adult.[2]

It is rather doubtful that this was the result of a lack of skill on the part of the artist. More likely, it was due to the fact that the child had no recognized place in the medieval world. This does not mean that he was not loved or well taken care of. He was simply not accounted for. Early youth was considered a period of innocence that passed quickly and was just as quickly forgotten.[3]

The families living in one dwelling were usually large. It was common for the extended family, aunts, uncles, grandparents, even servants, to live with the nuclear family. A child in this situation could easily be taken care of by others if his mother were not available. In a study of medical advice on child rearing from 1550 to 1900, Alice Ryerson shows that during the 1500's the child's dependency was given considerable encouragement. The swaddled baby was under constant attention and care. Mothers were greatly encouraged to nurse their babies. The child's cry was quickly responded to by either his being picked up and rocked, or breastfed. The child was allowed to remain in his mother's bed until he was weaned from the breast at around the age of two. But the weaning process was gradual. When he did finally move out of his parents' room, he was expected to move into a bed with his siblings or a servant. The gradual transition phase of this period closely resembles the earlier-mentioned phase that most societies hold or held.[4]

The great historical novel, *Kristin Lavrensdatter*, which is set in Norway around 1300 A.D., makes frequent mention of co-family sleeping customs. Around the thirteenth century, children entered the family portraits appearing more graceful and picturesque; a little closer to the modern concept of childhood.[5] During the fifteenth century a change took place. The "child" was discovered. And from then on, although slowly at first, he became the puppet of child educators who made it their business to decide, in every aspect, what was best for him. These men were primarily moralists rather than humanists.

Youth's innocence was questioned. And the advice was given, although still far ahead of the times, that co-family sleeping and touching each other might lead to promiscuity. Girson (who, according to Aries, was the first representative of this "modern" thought) suggests, however, only that "it would be a good thing" for children to start sleeping apart. He dared give no more than this suggestion because it was an overall custom for families to sleep together.[6]

Bedrooms as separate sleeping rooms were rare. For most people, the bed was thought of as precisely what it is—a more or less comfortable place to sleep, usually built into the wall, or free-standing with a curtain that could be drawn around it.[7]

During the reign of Louis XII in the fifteenth century, the French designed a bed of such beauty for the king that he held court and issued edicts from his *lit de justice*. The French nobility followed suit,

and began formally entertaining their guests from high, elegant, elabo-
rately canopied beds.[8] In the Victoria and Albert Museum in London,
England, a bed called "The Great Bed of Ware" is on display. It is
carved from oak and was reputed to sleep eleven couples in the last
quarter of the 16th century.

But among the common people, the room in which the sleeping
usually took place was either the large family kitchen, or another room
in which other daily activities also took place. It is not an unusual
scene in the paintings of 1500-1600 to see a family activity in the
foreground, and, as part of the furniture, a four-poster, curtained-off
bed in the background.

During the sixteenth century in England, the so-called Trinity bed
was developed. It consisted of a large bed upon which the immediate
family slept. Two smaller beds, often referred to as trundle beds, rolled
out from underneath the large bed. The older children, servants, or
relatives slept on this.[9]

In the seventeenth century, perhaps the largest of all beds was
designed by John Fosbrooke for the royal family. It could sleep 102
persons! Obviously, the "luxury" of separate beds and bedrooms of
which we boast today was not at all considered to be a sign of wealth
or prosperity during that time.

The attitude toward sex varies according to the accepted moral laws
of the people. The gestures, jokes, and sexual activities that took place
during the 1600's without regard for the children's presence would
shock the modern reader.[10] However, the child under the age of adolescence was believed to be unaware of or indifferent to sex. This further
explains why co-family sleeping created no problems. Whatever took
place was morally accepted, and the children were reared accordingly.[11]
"There is no written evidence," writes Ryerson, "that there were pro-
hibitions against masturbation, nudity, or sex play among children or
against the sexual stimulation of children by adults."[12]

Leaving a period that considered youth as something "only time
can cure," we note the appearance of a new concept in childhood.
The child is considered to be of psychological interest, and in the
1700's we begin to see a definite change in the approach to child
rearing and in the sleeping habits of the people as a whole.

A real propaganda campaign was launched to try to eradicate the
age-old custom of sleeping several in a bed. Throughout the eighteenth
century the advice was repeated that, besides the married couple, it

was indecent to go to bed with any other person, especially one of the opposite sex. Parents were urged to teach their children to conceal their bodies from one another.[13]

In the eighteenth century it was assumed that the child was not ready for life without special and proper treatment and education. The family became the modern concept of "the family;" namely, an institution in which the child receives his first preparation for adulthood and society. The child had taken a central place in his family. Educators, churchmen, and other professionals would, from now on, be concerned with arguing over what views of formal and moral education would be best suited for him.[14] The affluent family began to be concerned with privacy. Houses were built with specific bedrooms, therefore creating places for retreat and isolation.[15]

A medical textbook of the early 1800's suggests that, if possible, the nursery (which was the sleeping quarters of the children, not only of the newborn) should consist of two rooms. This would insure that while one was being used, the other could be ventilated. Pure air was greatly stressed. Furthermore, the nursery should have a high ceiling, tight windows, be spacious, perfectly dry, and receive much sunshine.[16] It is rather obvious that the advice considered only the wealthy few.

But before the steady decline of co-family sleeping gained full momentum, it enjoyed one final triumph. The custom of bundling came nearest to being a world-wide custom, including its practice in America, during the period from 1750-1780.[17] The usual definition of bundling is a man and woman lying on the same bed with their clothes on. They may be either conversing or sleeping. Usually, they were covered with a blanket or quilt.[18]

The majority of dwellings of the eighteenth century were small and, as in the case of the American settlers, many consisted of only one or two rooms in which the family lived and slept.[19] Frequently there were only one or two beds in the house. The scarcity of fuel had to be considered. It became, therefore, only common courtesy to invite a visitor, who was forced to stay overnight, to sleep with the rest of the family.

Husbands and parents frequently permitted travelers to bundle with their wives and daughters, even if the husband were not at home. Martha Washington mentions quite matter-of-factly in her diary the number of times she slept with strangers while the President was away.[20] Since it was rather unpleasant to sit together during the colder part of the year without a fire, it was considered proper courtesy that a gentleman should ask his lady friend to bundle.

This practice was even accepted among the sex-conscious Puritans, who would never have allowed such a practice to prevail had it proven to be a subtle cover-up for sex. Rather, it was stressed time and again that promiscuity and babies were not so much a result of bundling, as of the presence of a sofa or some other suitable place where lovers could retire in private.

"Going to bed" or "sleeping together" has thus not always had the connotation of "having sex," as the implication so frequently is today. But extra precautions were sometimes taken. In the Pennsylvania Dutch country, any possible over-enthusiasm between maid and lad was securely squelched by Mother's tying them each in a separate sack that was sealed with sealing wax. She then bid the pair a pleasant good night.[21]

Others did not go to such an extreme, but the use of a center board that kept the parties separated was quite common. That this practice was innocently accepted by all visitors is, of course, to be doubted. Indeed there were those who were quite bewildered when the host suggested that the guest share the family bed.

An example of this attitude may be read in a letter from Lieutenant Anbury, a British officer, who served in America during the Revolutionary War. His letter gives an interesting account of the manners and customs of that period.

The following epistle was dated at Cambridge, New England, November 20, 1777.[22]

> The night before we came to this town (Williamstown, Massachusetts) being quartered at a small log hut, I was convinced in how innocent a view the Americans look upon that indelicate custom they call bundling. Though they have remarkable good feather beds, and are extremely neat and clean, still I preferred my hard mattress, and being accustomed to it; this evening, however, owing to the badness of the roads, and the weakness of my mare, my servant had not arrived with my baggage at the time for retirement to rest. There being only two beds in the house, I inquired which I was to sleep in, when the old woman replied, "Mr. Ensign, our Jonathan and I will sleep in this,

and our Jemima and you shall sleep in that." I was much astonished at such a proposal and offered to sit up all night, when Jonathan immediately replied, "Oh, la! Mr. Ensign, you won't be the first man our Jemima has bundled with, will it, Jemima?" When little Jemima, who, by the by, was a very pretty, black-eyed girl of about sixteen or seventeen, answered, "No, Father, not by many, but it will be with the first Brittainer (the name they give to Englishmen). In this dilemma what could I do? The smiling invitation of pretty Jemima, thee, ye lips, the—Lord He' Mercy, where am I going to? But where ever I may be going to, I did not go to bundle with her—in the same room with her father and mother, my kind host and hostess too!

I thought of that. I thought of more besides—to struggle with the passions of nature, to clasp Jemima in my arms—to do nothing! For if amid all these temptations, the lovely Jemima had melted into kindness,

Nineteenth-century bedding.

she had been an outcast from the world, treated with contempt, abused by violence, and left perhaps to perish! No, Jemima; I could have endured all this to have been blest with you but it was too vast a sacrifice, when you was to be the victim! Suppose how great the test of virtue must be, or how cold the American constitution, when the unaccountable custom is in hospitable repute and perpetual practice.

According to Ryerson, there were probably three kinds of influences that accounted for the drastic change in child rearing practices, which took place during the nineteenth century.

During the latter part of the 1700's, and the first part of the 1800's, there was a strong religious movement that stressed the importance of personal communion with God and of the Christian perfection of the individual. "Both of these virtues depended on self-reliance," writes Ryerson, "a quality it was said best taught by early independence training."[23] A cry was heard over the country against bundling. It was in the form of a ballad, "A Poem Against Bundling; Dedicated to Ye Youth of Both Sexes."[24]

Hail giddy youth, inclined to mirth
To guilty amours prone,
Come blush with me, to think and see
How shameless you are grown.

'Tis not amiss to court and kiss,
Nor friendship do we blame,
But bundling in, women with men,
Upon the bed of shame;

And there to lay till break of day,
And think it is no sin,
Because a smock and petticoat
Have chanced to lie between.

The attitude toward sex and touching which, writes Aries, we would now consider to be bordering on perversion, became laden with sin. Earlier and earlier independence was sought in the child. Toilet training was to begin at between three weeks and six months. The child was expected to be reliably dry at night by the age of three. Punishment was sometimes recommended for failures in cleanliness.

All aspects of sexual behavior in children; e.g. masturbation and sex play among children, were strongly forbidden. Medical writers

emphatically disapproved of rocking and singing, handling and cuddling, and the immediate response to a young child's cry. The newborn
was still to sleep with his mother, but before he was a year old, he
had to be moved from her room to an *unshared* bed. [25] Feeding schedules
were introduced, and the age for weaning was reduced to approximately
nine months. Pacifiers and thumb-sucking were explicitly forbidden.

These changes represent a clear trend toward disapproval of dependent behavior. The idea of "teach him early independence or he will
be forever dependent" thus had its first stronghold, which has lasted
well into this decade.

In the book *The Unnatural History of the Nanny*, Gathorne-Hardy
postulates his view that the English Nanny was also of great influence
in changing child rearing practices during the 1800's. Many of the
eating and sleeping behaviors that we expect from children today were
instigated by the Nanny. In many families she was an extremely pow-
erful person, who completely took over the rearing of the children.

Another change that may have had considerable influence on child
rearing practices was the change from one family pattern to another.
As mentioned before, families were large and included the nuclear
family, the extended family, plus several servants all living in one
household. With the Industrial Revolution, and later the invention
of faster public transportation, families began to drift apart geographi-
cally. During the 1800's the large family began to be replaced by the
nuclear family, in which only parents and their children lived together.
Aunts and grandmothers were no longer available to relieve Mother
of her child rearing chores. She now had to resume full responsibility.
With less help, and therefore less time to spend with each child,
independence became a virtue for very practical reasons. The more
the child could do for himself, the less time Mother had to spend with
him, and the more pleased Mother was likely to be, especially since
she was now the only companion her husband could turn to.

Ryerson found no mention of the temper tantrum prior to 1800.
"This may mean that people were more tolerant of children's aggression
or perhaps that children were less aggressive at a time when repression
and adult control were not yet characteristic of training in the oral,
anal, and sexual spheres." This does not necessarily mean, of course,
that temper tantrums are primarily the result of oral, anal, and sexual
repression.

The increase in scientific knowledge during the eighteenth and nineteenth centuries also had an obvious effect on child rearing advice. Although the germ theory of disease was a much later scientific development, doctors of this period realized that certain illnesses were mysteriously associated with dirt. Once this connection was made, it was reasonable that cleanliness should assume a new and crucial significance.[26] This presumably led to the belief that separate sleeping was more hygienic than co-family sleeping.

In 1893, *Scribner's Magazine* carried what was probably the first twin-bed advertisement to appear in the United States. It read: "Our English cousins are now sleeping in separate beds. The reason is: *never breathe the breath of another.*"[27]

Thus the nineteenth century had set the stage for a type of sterile child rearing which, hopefully, will not re-occur again. Within a hundred years or so, child rearing practices had changed more drastically than perhaps ever before. Unfortunately, these changes did not end in themselves. With natural body drives and needs curtailed, new and other child rearing problems emerged. Problems that had not been present before, or had been minor, now needed special attention. The expert child educators came quickly to the foreground to give their advice on infant nutrition, on the child who "clung" to his mother, the child who cried, the child who balked at early weaning, the child who would not go to sleep by himself, the child who grew up into an adult with psychopathological problems.

Women's magazines and books on child rearing gradually took over the role of giving advice that Grandmother had occupied until now.[28]

Around 1900 almost all childbirths still occurred at home with the husband, a midwife, and perhaps other members of the family in attendance. By 1940, this aspect of the family's intimate home experience had also been taken away and most mothers delivered in hospitals. Even the immediate family was now removed.[29]

As soon as the child was born he was taken out of the hands of his parents and put into the conditioning regimen of society. Emotional intervention by the parents was frowned upon. The custom of separating mother and child at birth began around this time, presumably because many mothers, drugged at birth, were incapable of taking care of their infants for the first few days postpartum. Thus, the hospital nursery was instituted.

With the demonstrable successes of science and technology in other fields, behavioral psychologists, led by Dr. John Watson, decided to turn their backs on such unmeasurable qualities as motives, emotions, and aspirations. To the behaviorists, the development of the child was shaped entirely by the habits he acquired through contact with his environment.[30]

Emphatic advice was given that, in order to assure the child's development of "true" independence, mothers should not rock, cuddle, or kiss their babies too much. The perplexed mother of the 1920's, who was no longer allowed, or perhaps didn't even know how, to follow her own natural instinct, was now encouraged to turn to a child rearing book that was *the* Dr. Spock book of her time: *The Care and Feeding of Children,* by Dr. Emmett Holt.

One can hardly imagine more inhumane advice for a happy mother to rear a "happy" child. Baby must sleep alone in his own room. He must never be picked up when he is crying unless there seems to be some noticeable reason. It is necessary for Baby to cry loud and strong even if he gets red in the face. He should never be allowed to develop the habit of crying in order to be picked up and rocked, or of sucking or "any other such indulgence."[31] Discipline was best started in the first few weeks of life.

The trusting mother, intent on doing the "best" for her baby, stood by, frequently crying herself. One grandmother told me how she used to sit at the bottom of the stairs, crying, while her little baby was upstairs in his bassinet, crying.

The child had indeed become a major concern of the family, but he was untouchable. He was moved farther and farther away from the loving arms of his parents. Bottles took the place of Mother's breasts. Cribs took the place of the family bed. Playpens and strollers took the place of his parents' arms. Schedules took the place of Mother's intuition. Aloofness took the place, or at least was strongly urged to take the place, of parents' indulging love.

The child was alone in the midst of it all.

Not only was the child removed from the intimacy of the family, but Mother, too, was dethroned and replaced by the maidenly (not matronly), liberated (without a child in her arms), free-going (replaced by gadgets) woman. A few decades later, Ashley Montagu wrote his book, *The Natural Superiority of Women,* which could be summed up in one sentence: "Hey, look who you really are!"

During this time the use of single beds became widespread. Medical advice stressed the idea of separate beds and the importance of "hygiene." Although the exact type of hygiene desired was rarely mentioned, the factor of communicable diseases may have played an important part.[32] Indeed, I have questioned whether there is a connection between medical discoveries of communicable diseases (with their stress on minimizing the chance of "catching" some illness from someone else), and the obvious success child psychiatrists *et al* had in convincing parents not to indulge their children. The less one touched, or was touched, the less chance there was of giving or receiving some horrible illness. By this time the myth, "It is dangerous to sleep with your baby," had become widespread, and further persuaded mothers to have their babies sleep by themselves.

During the 1940's a large array of sleep aids became available, judging from the bedroom business. One could now buy sleep masks, ear stops, knee pillows, sinus masks, chin straps, ear warmers, and recordings of soporific music. Some people even put the earpieces of a stethoscope in their ears and the receiver on their hearts. The sounds of their own steadily beating hearts apparently soothed them and helped them to fall asleep.[33] These gadgets, however, were only subtle substitutes for another's warm, soothing, and relaxing companionship.

During this time the "only child" family became popular. Should this be any wonder? What mother and father would want to have more children and not be allowed to touch them?

Families were smaller now, and houses were built with three or four bedrooms. Each child could have his own room. Individual bedrooms were no longer the exceptions. They became necessities.

In the 1950's, another change took place. A few publications concerned with child rearing suggested that it is all right for young children to spend some time in their parents' bed.[34] Fathers were beginning to see a glimpse of their children just after they were born. The need for more information about breastfeeding resulted in the birth of La Leche League. And articles began to appear suggesting that a crying baby is an unhappy baby who needs comforting.

Some individual natural childbirth classes were given during the 1950's. As word and enthusiasm spread, it was decided that some type of organization would be formed to stimulate communication among isolated efforts. In 1954 the Milwaukee Childbirth Association was formed, and in 1960 the International Childbirth Education Association came into being at a convention in the same city.

Until mid-1900, the Euro-American industrial culture tended to consider the emotional commitments and care of babies to be mostly a female role. This was also changing, however, as Father now moved closer to the baby by being present at the birth. He also seemed to take more demonstrable pride and joy in caring for his offspring. We now see fathers pushing strollers, feeding babies, carrying infants on their backs in infant carriers, walking unhappy, teething babies. However, I fear that some men and women are confused about the role of the father, and believe that he may not only be a mother-substitute at times, but a mother-replacement as well. No one can replace Mother. Also, no one can replace Father. Each holds his or her *own significant* place in the child's life.

By 1970 Ashley Montagu's book, *Touching: The Human Significance of the Skin,* became a best seller. Throughout the book, he speaks highly of co-family sleeping.

By 1982 a mother wrote: "Our last child was born with the assistance of her Daddy. She was nursed in the delivery room and came with us to our room shortly after being checked over briefly in the nursery. Then followed the long, leisurely love-in that I had instinctively wanted with our other five children but never had. This was the first baby I was allowed to hold in my arms for many hours after birth. I know I shall always treasure that beautiful time, a little bit of heaven. During the next two-and-a-half days, Jeanie cried very little, nursing gently, frequently, and completely on her own schedule. I had her in my room all day, and on demand at night, which often meant that she slept in my bed for several hours. I was supremely content and happy, and so was our baby."

After Mother and Baby came home from the hospital, the infant was welcomed into the family bed, which was frequently visited by other children in the family as well.

We seem to be approaching the end, or rather the beginning, of a full circle. In ancient times, the whole family slept together. Babies were carried around, breastfed, and taken care of when in need. They were generally accepted without much further thought. During the early Middle Ages, the child was still of no particular account in his own right, but during the seventeenth and eighteenth centuries he was beginning to be noticed as someone who had to be molded. Early independence was stressed. Separation of family members became fashionable.

Although the center of attention by 1900, the child was taken away from the emotional unit, the family. Inventions of every kind of mother-substitute imaginable inundated the parents of the 1930's and '40's.

By the 1950's, articles on the big generation gap and the lack of respect that youth had for its parents appeared in many a publication. The need for psychiatrists, psychologists, counselors multiplied.

The 1960's arrive. Young parents express dissatisfaction with childbirth and child rearing practices of the previous generation. Prepared childbirth, breastfeeding, and a loving, understanding approach to offspring gain popularity. Family unity is stressed by child rearing publications and groups such as La Leche League. Parents are encouraged to stay "in touch" with their children. The young child is slowly returning to the bosom of the family.

The first edition of this book came out in 1976. Shortly afterwards, talk shows on radio and television began discussing where children should sleep. As was to be expected at first, co-family sleeping was viciously attacked. But that, too, is changing. Perhaps man's innate arrogance and feeling of superiority over nature is changing as he takes a more humble look at the scheme and wisdom of life and how it all fits together. It would be beneficial to study nature carefully. It's been around a lot longer than the fleeting passage of each generation.

7

Some Anthropological Observations

To be human is to be aware of the feelings of other human beings.

For some time now, anthropologists, doctors, and others have made intensive studies of societies that have received little or no influence from modern Western civilization. Such people live as close to nature as their environment dictates and are not affected by the mechanical, scientific, and research-oriented world. It has been observed that these groups are not infrequently in remarkably good health, both physically and emotionally.

Eric Ericson, the noted psychoanalyst, advises us that we should study the child rearing systems of other societies. Contrary to our rather superior convictions of the unerring ways of our child rearing practices, Ericson says that their methods are far from primitive, and frequently of such integrity that we should envy them.[1]

If the child rearing methods of the past 150 years had resulted in great improvement over previous methods in rearing happy, emotionally-stable people, we might do well to study and apply them. However, there is no evidence of such superior results. As a matter of fact, there seems to be more an indication toward the contrary. The concept of separate sleeping arrangements is of such new vintage that it has not yet had a chance to stand the test of time. The test seems to be on rather shaky grounds. Parents are repeatedly bombarded by yet another book on child rearing, another approach, each claiming to have *the* answer. The change is constant. Confusion and frustration persist. It would be of interest, therefore, in the light of anthropological observations, to look at the types of sleeping arrangements in which people have engaged for thousands of years.

It must again be emphasized, of course, that sleeping together is not going to solve the problems we are confronted with in our tremendously complex world. By reviewing what other peoples do, and by observing the effect on the individual, we may, however, rediscover how best to equip men with inner strength.

Travelling with his movie camera throughout the world, Hans Hass has shown that many of our human traits, emotional behavior, actions and reactions, and behavior patterns are the same in all men.[2] Sickness and death bring as much sadness and grief to the Bushman as they do to us. Happiness is as much valued by the Arapesh family in New Guinea as in our own family. The need to find comfort in fellow human beings, and for emotional fulfillment, is universal.[3]

In a study by the anthropologist Whiting, it was stated that in forty-eight out of fifty-six societies studied, babies slept with their mothers for at least the first year of life. In twenty-four of these societies, the baby slept between the mother and father.[4] In another crosscultural study by Barry and Paxson, in which 186 different cultures were studied, not one culture reported Mother and Father sleeping in a separate room from the baby. In the majority of these cultures, the mother slept with the baby. The father's sleeping proximity varied among the groups. He may have slept in the same bed, or the same room, but sometimes in a different building.[5] These statistics are not as vivid as actual anthropological accounts, however.

In his book, *Fear: Contagion and Conquest,* Dr. James Moloney reports on the Okinawan Indians. He writes that from birth until age six, the young children sleep between their mother and father. The baby always sleeps next to his mother on the same mat. When the pre-schooler reaches school age, he is moved to another room to sleep with his older brothers and sisters. Sexual relationship between the parents is not hidden from the children.

The young child enjoys unrestricted breastfeeding and in the event that he is put down, he is immediately picked up and nursed again whenever he begins to cry. Without the restrictions of cumbersome clothing and the taboos of an exposed breast, nursing is much simpler and need not necessarily interfere with what the Okinawan mother is doing. The Okinawan child is not corporally punished. He is not "toilet trained." He is bowel and bladder educated after he becomes old enough to realize what is expected of him. The child is not frustrated, and should his mother not be immediately available when he cries, an aunt, grandmother, or friend comforts the youngster. The youngster thus receives love, security, tenderness, and closeness not only from his immediate family but from others around him as well.

This, Dr. Moloney feels, is the key to the great inner security the Okinawan person has. He says, "The Okinawan adult not only walks with emotional stability, but with tranquility, with contentment, with pride, with a sense of well-being, with love—all of which stems from this basic security he received from his infancy." Dr. Moloney goes so far as to say that, after almost a year and a half of close contact with these people, he has never seen more emotionally-stable, magnificently-integrated adults.[6]

Margaret Mead, in her study of the Balinese child, writes in her account that the youngster spends most of his first few years in the arms or on the back of another human being. The close proximity of other bodies is enjoyed during sleep. As adults, these people fall asleep quite easily while leaning against other persons. The touch of another person induces relaxation.[7] Few have observable hang-ups about sex and homosexuality is almost unheard of.

The Japanese family sleeps together, and so does the African Bushman. Also, the Korean child sleeps with his mother.[8] Families all over the world sleep together.

While in the Philippines, Helen Wessel, author of *Natural Childbirth and the Family,* stayed with a doctor, his wife, and seven children. The youngest, who was seven, was still sleeping with her parents every night. She slept between them, closer to the father so the mother could rest, they explained. It was a warm, loving family. Mrs. Wessel was particularly impressed by the fact that the children, most of them teen-aged, *never* quarreled! Mrs. Wessel's daughter, a Peace Corps woman who lived there two years, said she never once heard any of them quarrel. The older children shared rooms and beds, boys with boys, girls with girls. A number of American parents have also definitely noticed a reduction in sibling quarreling when the children sleep together.

The emphasis in child rearing by the African community, reports Breetveld, is on teaching the child that he is an integral part of the family unit, and giving him a deep-rooted feeling of belonging. They stress a man-to-man rather than a man-to-object relationship. The young child is rarely out of the arms of another person during his first few years of life.[9]

It is believed that the Eskimo's ability to keep such an amiable disposition, even though his environment can place him under extremely stressful conditions, is due to the minimum lack of frustration that is placed upon him as a child. A close unity exists within his family. The very young child is almost constantly carried on his mother's back, and is nursed freely. Since their igloos are quite warm, the Eskimos usually sleep in the nude in close bodily contact with each other.[10] Foreigners who have lived among them have remarked how delightful and happy the children and grown-ups of the far North are, how secure and well-integrated the adult personalities. Missionaries who have lived among them to teach the Christian religion have been known to say that it was not the Eskimos who needed reformation but the white men.[11]

Due to Western influence, however, many of the natural customs of the above-mentioned societies are, unfortunately, rapidly changing. The customs referred to existed at the time of observation and recording, but do not necessarily exist at the present.

The fascinating difference between the Mundugumor and the Arapesh tribes is given by Margaret Mead in her book, *From the South Seas*. The Arapesh people are extremely gentle, loving, and trusting. They love children, and a mother will suckle her infant whenever he cries. She does not concern herself with schedules or whether the child may or may not be hungry. The child cries, the mother picks him up, and if he so wants, she nurses him. Through her ongoing attempt to soothe the uncomfortable child, he learns first to trust his mother completely, and later his other fellow tribesmen. The child is allowed to wean when he is ready. He sleeps with his parents.

The Mundugumor people are exactly the opposite. They despise the pregnant woman. When a child is born, he is placed in a hard, uncomfortable basket. He is nursed only when he simply will not stop crying. His mother stands while she nurses him, and as soon as he stops sucking, if only for a second, the baby is put down. Instead of letting the child wean when he is ready, the security-seeking child is pushed away from his mother. She forces him to wean long before he is ready, but at a time when he can survive on other foods.

These people lack all trust in one another. Until the government outlawed it, they actively practiced head-hunting. They are hateful and distrustful. Sexual foreplay is performed with biting and scratching one's partner to the point of bleeding.[12]

Anthropological studies reveal that among those societies which seem to produce happy, emotionally-stable people, co-family sleeping, unrestricted breastfeeding, and almost constant physical contact with the children in their early years is the custom. (Thus a complete fulfillment of the transition phase, as has been discussed earlier in this book.) This cannot be stressed strongly enough. Funded scholarly studies are now discovering the same!

A baby's need for breast milk, the best infant nutrition there is; his need for sleeping next to his family members, the best form of security there is; his need to be comforted by another human being, the best comforter there is—these are the needs of children the world over.

8

The Infant

Bitter are the tears of a child:
Sweeten them.
Deep are the thoughts of a child:
Quiet them.
Sharp is the grief of a child:
Take it from him.
Soft is the heart of a child:
Do nothing to harden it.

Lady Pamela Wyndham Glenconner
"A Child"

"Why do people smile when they see a hospital nursery full of crying babies? One close look at the intensity with which each tiny creature painfully declares his own inborn awareness that something is horribly wrong should wrench our hearts. Deprived of every newborn's birthright to the presence of his mother's warm body and soothing, spontaneous nursing, most hospital-born babies' first experiences are ones of stress rather than warm, loving mothering." (Lucy Cutler) Here is the frustrated, concerned cry of a young mother.

Is there really any bona fide justification for this separation, or is it an antiquated practice, a result of socially- and medically-oriented events? Is it really necessary for Mother and Baby to be separated after birth, especially in the light of our present-day medical knowledge?

Most babies were once born in the family bed, at home, and slept there until they joined their siblings. Perhaps they spent the first few months in a cradle before sleeping in a bed; nonetheless, they were usually near their mother.[1] The infant was breastfed shortly after birth, and frequently thereafter whenever he cried.

Today's practice is drastically different. Many hospitals have an arbitrary rule as to how soon after birth a mother "may" have *her* baby. This may be anywhere from six hours to as long as a day.

71

Soon after birth, a baby is quickly shown to the mother, then whisked off to the central nursery (which has been referred to by a prominent doctor as nothing more than a "place for displaced persons"). There, his weight, length, physical characteristics, and any other traits are recorded. A name and/or number band is placed around his wrist, and he is then put into a bassinet alongside other bassinets.[2]

Gone is the warm, soothing world where no cold, no hunger, no stillness, no loneliness existed. Gone is the heartbeat and the voice so familiar to him. Gone is his mother.

And the mother, who for many months continually felt the presence of that new life, whose arms ache to hold that which her womb no longer carries, whose breasts are full of rich milk for her baby, is left separated, void, and alone. Gone is her child. "Gone at a time," says Montagu, "when a continuing development of the symbiotic relationship is so necessary for the further development of both of them."[3]

Our society tends to ignore or belittle a woman's emotions toward her unique biological functions.[4] The mother is told that her baby is in the nursery so that she can rest and be free from the burden of having to take care of her child. But with telephone calls, paperboys, clean-up ladies, and nurses coming and going, how many mothers have actually found their hospital stay restful? Added to these disturbances is the anxiety, "Is that *my* baby crying in the nursery?"

Even the makers of paper diapers are aware of the mother's desire to hold her infant. But to make matters worse, they exploit this feeling and use it in advertising. One diaper advertisement expressed it:

> A newborn baby spends so little time in his mother's arms. And yet so much time in diapers. Now that he is born you would just love to hold him. But he can't be in your arms all the time you want…

Baby and mother are an emotional unit. It hurts to be separated. Baby cries because he needs his mother. Mother peers anxiously at her infant because she needs to give relief, but the glass window of the nursery separates the two. They both know what is right, but are told they are wrong.[5]

Much research is now being done in the field of the mother-infant relationship. A growing amount of clinical observations suggests that the degree of contact they enjoy, and the kind of environment the child is exposed to immediately after delivery, might strongly influence this relationship.[6]

The late Dr. Raymond Albrecht, one of the pioneers in father-participated childbirth, stated, "I'm confident that when the mother and father relate to the baby immediately after birth, somehow or other data is put in his computer. He understands in some way. This is data that will be in the brain forever."[7] This is called imprinting, a word coined by the German naturalist Konrad Lorenz, who made the statement that once imprinting has taken place it can be neither erased nor reversed.[8]

Birth and the Family Journal of 1973 reported on the research of Dr. Marshall Klaus in an editorial. He observed the interpersonal relationship between mothers and their infants during the first few hours after birth and when the children were two years of age. Babies were observed to focus their eyes better in the first hours after birth than in the next few days. They also responded well to the high-pitched voices that mothers often use. The mothers touched and stroked their babies a great deal. After two years, it was noticed that those mothers who had been allowed undisturbed contact with their babies at birth used more gentle clarification and comfort with their toddlers than did the control mothers, who were denied early contact with their infants. They also seemed to have greater rapport with their children, the article concluded.

When held in someone's arms, infants just a few hours old will frequently stare and stare into the eyes of that person. The imprinting that takes place will be a part of the infant forever. Shouldn't this first impression or imprint be as beautiful as possible? And what face is more beautiful than that of a new mother looking at her own birth gift?

A mother and her newborn baby have every right to be together from birth on. This can make a significant contribution toward producing a trusting individual capable of warm, close relationships. Both Mother and Child have a need for reciprocal stimulation which should not be interfered with. Yet, the greatest interference of all is placed upon them. Separation. The reasons for this separation are now being questioned.

The first interference with the mother-child relationship usually comes when the neonate is not allowed to nurse directly following birth. Now some doctors feel that, apart from the emotional benefits of placing Baby immediately in his mother's arms and allowing him to touch her, this may definitely be better for him and his mother *physically*.

Immediate and frequent nursing drastically reduces the chance of engorgement of the breast. Nursing also stimulates the uterus to contract, which hastens the separation of the placenta and the uterus. This in turn helps to close the blood vessels in the part of the uterus to which it was attached, thus reducing the chance of post-delivery hemorrhaging. It also hastens the return of the uterus to the non-pregnant state. Early breastfeeding is used by some doctors to express a reluctant placenta or to check excessive bleeding.[9]

The great beneficial effects of breastfeeding were brought to the attention of a young mother, who told me about an experience she had.

Several hours after the birth of her second daughter, born at home, her first child playfully fell on her mother's abdomen. Shortly thereafter the mother began to have strong and irregular contractions. These resembled the contractions of the last stages of labor. After some time with no improvement, the midwife was contacted. The mother was advised to start nursing her newborn immediately. Quite soon after placing the infant to the breast, the contractions became regular. Mother stayed in bed with her baby nursing and dozing on and off. After a while a clot was expelled, and, although tender for some time in the abdominal region, the mother began to feel better.

In the La Leche League reprint, "On Nursing the Newborn . . . How Soon?", it is stated that the sucking reflex is at its height twenty to thirty minutes after birth. If the infant is not nursed, the reflex diminishes rapidly only to reappear again about two days later. On the other hand, if the infant is breastfed soon after birth and frequently thereafter, he takes the breast well and the early physiologic loss of weight is minimized.

Apparently, not all babies nurse well immediately following birth. These babies lick the nipple for some time before actually settling down to nurse. However, even more important is that the baby be allowed to touch, smell, and perhaps in other forms unknown to us, establish contact with his mother. He will then nurse when he is ready.

The first milk, colostrum, is a valuable source of immunity and protection against various diseases and infections. The sooner Baby receives this first milk, the better it is for him. No substitutes can provide such protection. The amount of colostrum the baby ingests the first few times he nurses is small; thus, the chance of his choking is unlikely. As a matter of fact, colostrum seems to be an excellent substance for clearing and washing down the mucus.[10]

No sooner have Mother and Baby established initial contact, however, than they are faced with another possible separation. Baby is usually put into an artificially-heated bassinet, or wrapped in aluminum foil, or placed under a heat lamp. Recent reports seem to indicate that this common practice is unnecessary and may even be bad for the newborn.

There is no evidence that the full-term infant of a relatively unmedicated mother will suffer so much heat loss as to be harmful to him. As a matter of fact, studies from Sweden, Finland, and Switzerland indicate that the results from the slight cooling are good because a cooled brain consumes less oxygen than a warmed brain. Thus, there is less danger of oxygen deprivation.[11]

Experiences by Yale-New Haven Hospital in Connecticut and by the late Dr. Raymond Albrecht indicate that, when wrapped in a pre-warmed blanket and placed in the arms of his mother, the temperature of the neonate remained stable. The slight cold stress immediately following birth before the temperature stabilizes may act as a stimulus to the onset of respiration in a healthy, vigorous baby.

Likewise, the act of touching is known to stimulate Baby's breathing mechanism and, writes Ribble, "enables the whole respiratory process to become organized under the control of his own nervous system."[12]

Bathing is another practice that has been subject to controversy in the last few decades. It is believed by some doctors that the vernix caseosa (the cream-like substance with which many newborns are covered) has beneficial properties, as it protects the infant from superficial infections and acts as an insulating layer against heat loss and the penetration of too much cold.[13]

During the Second World War, the *vernix* was purposely left on, to be absorbed into the skin. It was a time of scarcity, a time that necessitated the utilization of every resource. When left on, the *vernix*, like a cold cream, is simply absorbed into the skin, or rubbed off on clothing, usually within one to two hours.

It is rather ironic that, because of such concern for heat loss, the baby is first placed in a warmer, then washed, and then placed in the warmer again. While all this fuss is going on, Baby could have been sleeping peacefully with his mother and nursing.

Fortunately, however, times are changing. More and more hospitals are now attempting to turn the birth experience into a family affair. They offer *rooming-in*, a situation in which the mother has her child with her whenever she wishes except during visiting hours, or when situations arise that would prevent her from being with her baby.

The neonate is thus under the constant and watchful eye of his mother. With the hospital staff's reassurance of the woman's capabilities as a mother, the new couple may spend a few restful, blissful days together. Mother feels complete. Baby feels complete. In fact, together they make a complete unit.

The best place to have a baby is in the family bed at home. Unfortunately, a home birth situation is a service that has sadly lacked empathy from the American medical profession. But there seems to be a trend back to giving birth at home.

Having a baby at home can be safe, especially when the woman has had adequate prenatal care, has been educated to participate actively during parturition, and when there is a knowledgeable midwife or birth helper in attendance. Many civilized and technologically-advanced countries, such as Sweden and the Netherlands, have a far lower infant mortality rate than that of the United States. As a matter of course, these countries offer a choice between the hospital or home birth with skilled attendants.[14]

The well-researched and excellently-written booklet, *The Cultural Warping of Childbirth*, by Doris Haire, Co-president of the International Childbirth Education Association, is a source of information well worth reading. It provides a great deal of insight into why the United States continues to be outranked by fourteen other developed countries on the list of infant mortality rates. She points out a number of times when a more natural approach to childbirth, either for a home or hospital birth, is an important key in lowering the incidence of infant mortality and morbidity.

Haire emphasizes adequate prenatal education for training in management of labor, minimizing medication and use of obstetrical instruments, and educating the mothers with respect to the hazards involved when these measures, as well as elective induction of labor, are applied. She further stresses the importance of having a skilled midwife and a supportive member of the family present during labor and birth. She greatly encourages breastfeeding, particularly in the case of a premature birth.

"It may be convenient to blame our relatively poor infant outcome on a lack of facilities or inadequate governmental funding," says Mrs. Haire, "but it is obvious from the research being carried out that we could effect an immediate improvement in infant outcome by changing the pattern of obstetrical care in the United States."[15]

Dr. White of La Leche League said, "I think we are in a little danger in medicine of sometimes spoiling the experiences of healthy people because we are terribly worried about the rare cases."[16]

There is something special about a baby's being born in the warm, familiar bed at home. It gives the mother a sweet, complete feeling.

There is sufficient evidence indicating that premature babies do much better when they are handled and, if possible, nursed by their mothers.

At Stanford University School of Medicine, forty-one mothers were encouraged to handle their premature infants at any time of the day or night. There was no increase in the much-feared infections, and no complications of any sort were recorded. The benefits to everyone involved were considerable.[17]

It used to be thought that premature babies did much better on certain formulas than on breast milk, since they gained weight faster. But it has subsequently been discovered, reports Pryor, that the gain was a result of fluid retention in the tissues. The weight gain on breast milk may be slower at first, but it is a healthy gain[18] with a better hemoglobin level.[19]

La Leche League newsletters cite numerous incidents of mothers who have successfully nursed their premature babies. Some doctors even feel that it is possible—indeed desirable—to discharge premies from the hospital much earlier than is usually recommended, especially when they are coming home with a mother prepared to breastfeed her baby. The closeness possible at home is physically and emotionally important to both mother and child. For all intents and purposes, writes Janov, a premature baby is still a fetus, requiring all the love, warmth, and sensory stimulation provided by the womb.[20] It was concluded in a recent study that early discharge did not increase the risk of morbidity or mortality. (*LLL News,* 1972, p. 28.)

Some mothers of premature babies have instinctively felt that the close contact that the baby received after coming home and joining the family in bed helped to make up for the days or even weeks the infant spent alone. It also helped Mom to make up for the "baby-less" days and nights.

It is a human trait to be sociable and want to cuddle. This is even stronger in young children, especially when they are falling asleep. Perhaps they seek to recreate the warm, secure feeling of life *in utero.*[21]

Children have more difficulty falling asleep when separated from their mothers. Anna Freud said so. Mothers everywhere know so. This may not be the case if a child feels comfortable with a favorite article that serves as a mother substitute. But a breastfeeding mother knows that even though she may have nursed her child an hour before bedtime, he wants to nurse again as a means of relaxing and drifting off to sleep.

Nursing mothers may also notice that their breasts, especially the left one, pulsate gently with the beating of their hearts. The nursing baby will actually feel the heartbeat that he heard and felt before he was born. Breastfeeding has such a soothing effect on the child. Nursing means "to comfort," whether the baby experiences hunger, pain, tension, or loneliness; a need to suck, to feel, or to touch. Breastfeeding means more than feeding at the breast. The fact that Baby gets milk is almost incidental.

Should we have to "prove" that babies are more relaxed and better off when they are with their mothers? Dr. Lee Salk devised a machine that reproduced the human heartbeat. Hearing this, newborn babies slept better, were happier, and even gained weight faster, reports Salk, then those infants who spent their days in the customary hospital nursery.[22]

It is incredible that the importance of hearing the mother's heartbeat could have been so readily accepted and used by dog owners, but ignored until only recently for human babies. Most of us know that, when a puppy has been taken away from its mother, a loud clock (wrapped in a towel, as a surrogate for Mother) will quiet down the lonesome pup. But modern science has finally caught up with the dog owners. Mothers can now buy tapes and phonograph records, which can be played for their lonesome babies while they busy themselves with other things. The recordings play sounds from "a mother's womb, her heart, her main artery, and her veins"—as one recording claims, "familiar music from the baby's environment." It is to be desperately hoped that only a few parents will fall for this mechanical, degrading trap. What adult would passively accept a tape-recorded message of "I love you" sent by a loved one who chooses not to deliver his adoration in person?

After learning about all the "fabulous" inventions that serve as mother substitutes, but unfortunately bring with them their inevitable breakdowns, one doctor exclaimed, "Eureka! Why don't we use Mother?"

Some young babies, after falling asleep in their mother's arms, wake up the instant they are put down. As a solution to this problem, many mothers lie down with the child until he has fallen asleep. Then it is so easy to slip away from him without his awakening.

One of the most tender stories that was related to me was about a mother and her six-week-old infant. The baby had fallen asleep in his mother's arms, and was then laid on his parents' large bed. Not wanting to disturb the child, Mother lay down a few feet away from the little one, and also fell asleep. When she awoke, she found her baby curled up snugly against her. While Mother was asleep, the infant evidently maneuvered himself over to her, where he felt he belonged.

Whether during the day or at night, parents need not be afraid to pick up their child as soon as he starts to cry. We've heard a lot about spoiling little babies by picking them up the minute they cry, or how normal it is for them to "cry it out" for a while, or how healthy it is for the young infant to cry.

"The truth is," says Salk, "that by picking him up we are teaching him that someone responds to his needs, whether it is the need for physical sensation or for food."[23] When our response to a crying baby is inconsistent, we are teaching him that people are not trustworthy, and he may feel confused and powerless. The interesting thing is that young children, who have not yet been brainwashed, will immediately respond with concern to an unhappy baby. But as adults, we want a reason, an excuse, a label that we can attach to his crying: is he hungry, cold, frightened? As long as we have an explanation that satisfies us, we feel a lot better. Yet, haven't many adults experienced feelings of loneliness or rejection that have defied easy explanation? Of course.

Anthropologists have repeatedly reported one striking difference between babies in the Western world and babies in the pre-literate world. In the latter, babies seldom cry, and if they do, they are usually picked up immediately and nursed, or soothed in some other way. I need not comment on the crying of the Western baby. One hears it everywhere, and for longer than a few minutes, day after day until the baby is grown up and the cry becomes silent. You don't hear it so easily anymore. You can't soothe it so easily anymore.

In the early 1950's a study of infants was made in an American nursery. Observers, recording infants' behavior twenty-four hours a day, indicated that the average infant cried for almost two hours daily![24] Makes one wonder what kind of person could sit with pen and clock in hand and do nothing but observe another being intently unhappy, and notate the tears of loneliness and hurt in increments of minutes.

I was recently told by a mother who had delivered her baby in a hospital that she had overheard one nurse say to another, "We will have to put that one crying baby in the 'Naughty Baby Room.' He keeps waking the other babies up with his screaming and hollering."

The almost unfailing action with which animal mothers respond to their infants' cries; i.e., immediately going to and touching the young, should perhaps give us further insight into the importance of the immediate physical response to the cry. Indeed, reports Bowlby, it should be of serious concern to us that in our "advanced" and "civilized" society we should act in a way so utterly against this very basic natural behavior.[25]

"There is no harm in a child crying; the harm is done if his cries are not answered," says Dr. Salk.[26]

Crying is the infant's first form of social communication because it calls for a response by another person. He is sounding a distress signal to let others know he is in need of something.

Perhaps the feeling of utter desperation and loneliness that an infant who is left to cry must have may be best imagined by those who have had the misfortune of being totally dependent on others, such as during a hospital stay. When no one comes with a soothing word, a drink of water, a pain-relieving medicine, or some other response to a call, one tends to become bitter and lose faith in the people around him. If this happens once, the incident may be soon forgotten. But should this happen frequently, it would have an adverse effect.

It is disturbing that the interpretation of a baby's cry as a deliberate means to wrap us around his little finger and dominate us has been believed by so many people. Several mothers have told me that they loved holding their babies so much they could hardly wait for their infants to wake from a nap and begin crying, just so they could pick them up. In this light, the crying takes on a totally different meaning. The first interpretation shows a basic fear and distrust of the child; the second gives him credit for being a basically cooperating human being who must use a cry for communication until he learns to speak.

In his book, *Intimate Behavior*, Desmond Morris states that it is difficult to comprehend the warped tradition which says that it is better to leave a small baby to cry so that he does not "get the better of you."[27]

Instead of encouraging mothers to meet the baby's emotional needs, one doctor advocated using the "I'll-make-you-stop-crying" method. A mother of a nine-month-old baby (who cried a great deal and was in constant need of his mother's presence) called her doctor for advice.

He told her to ignore the child for three days, and not to pay special attention to him other than at feeding and bath times. If, after three days, the youngster did not stop crying and clinging, he would hospitalize the baby for three to four days. "This has always done the trick," said the doctor. (She did not follow his advice.)

There is an old Yiddish proverb that says, "Small children disturb your sleep; big children, your life." Dr. Herbert Ratner elaborated on this proverb in his Keynote address to the 1964 La Leche League International Convention.

> If we don't lose sleep over our children when they are young, we will lose sleep over them when they are old. Though it is easy to ignore an infant—he is a little thing, you can close the door on him, it seems to you to be a private matter since there are no witnesses around—just remember that it is not going to be as easy to ignore the cries of an older child, a child who gets into trouble with the law, a child who is a juvenile delinquent. Now it becomes a public matter, and you have a responsibility. So just remember in the middle of the night when you get up, not too joyously, to take care of the needs of your infant, that this is the natural time to have your sleep disturbed. It is going to be awfully grievous when, as a result of not permitting your sleep to be disturbed when your babies need you, your sleep is going to be disturbed in many more complicated ways when the child grows older.

Babies who still cry even after their mothers have "tried everything" can cause quite a bit of distress, especially during the night. The following suggestions as to the causes of and possible solutions to the problem of crying may be helpful.

A baby may become more fussy and demanding if he senses a feeling of resentment in the mother. Try, therefore, to enjoy those quiet night times together—they won't last forever. It would also help not to look at the clock when he awakens. Take off your watch. It is amazing how much the knowledge of the number of times and at what hours one was awakened can influence one's disposition.

We might consider it our right to have a good night's sleep. But, as Dr. White of the La Leche League Advisory Board and father of eleven children, said:

> A lot of people are so square as to think they're entitled to a night's sleep. Nobody is entitled to a full night's sleep, whether a parent or not, if someone needs her or him.

Let your baby know that he is loved unconditionally, that you would welcome him into your arms at any time.

With the kind permission of Jean Perkins, La Leche League Counselor, I have taken the following excerpts from her reprint, "Possible Causes of Crying and Frequent Nighttime Nursings."

- Baby could be hungry.
- Does he need burping?
- He may feel too warm or too cold.
- His diaper may need changing.
- He may feel tired.
- Perhaps he has been over-stimulated by light or noise.
- Is he bored? Being close to Mother or having bright things to watch can help.
- Has he been insecurely or roughly handled?
- Can you observe any signs of illness?
- He may be troubled from too much handling. (But not as likely as from too little.)
- Have there been great changes in his routine or people who have handled him?
- Personality plays a part—some babies just seem to cry more than others.
- He may need additional motion or rocking.
- He may need more consistent routine, or fewer outings until he is more mature.
- Baby may be noticing tension or insecurity in his mother—or problems or conflicts in the home.
- Teething may cause fussiness even before teeth appear above the gums.
- Especially sensitive babies may need to have their nursing routine adapted to them. (Example: only one breast per feeding.)
- He may be disturbed by substances eaten by the mother: drugs, certain foods, additives.
- He may be allergic to his formula or foods he eats directly.
- He may be allergic to environmental toxins, such as the fumes coming off furniture, clothing, perfumes.

Don't feel like a failure if Baby cries, but don't let him cry alone. Keep looking for other possible reasons for his distress.[28]

Some mothers have found that cupping their hand over the infant's head and applying slight pressure stops Baby's crying. Another mother found that blowing gently on Baby's head would quiet him down.

Dr. Niles Newton feels that perhaps one reason for crying may be Baby's missing the womb. In her reprint, "When Baby's Crying Becomes Trying," she comments that some mothers, especially breastfeeding mothers, "go back to the ways of their great-great-grandmothers when faced with a fussy baby at night." She refers to old medical textbooks, which emphasize the need for the infant to be comforted by sleeping with his mother.

She recommends:

> If the bed seems a bit crowded, consider a king-size bed. Some couples prefer to have a mattress on the floor for Mother and Baby while they sleep and nurse. When the baby goes to sleep, he is left on the mattress and Mother goes back to bed with her husband.

If a baby or child is especially restless during an illness, perhaps Father could sleep elsewhere for the night. Or Mother and Baby could rest in another room so as not to disturb other members of the family. I do believe that, even though both parents are responsible for rearing the children, it is only fair that Father, usually the breadwinner, gets his proper rest when possible. This certainly does not mean that he should not help out when needed. At times, his reassuring voice or touch can work wonders, especially in the middle of the night.

What is crying? Desmond Morris writes, "crying says, 'come here,' and smiling says, 'please stay.'"[29]

Breastfeeding mothers have noticed that they will frequently awaken in the middle of the night shortly *before* their baby begins to whimper. Results of recent research suggest, according to an article in a LLLI publication, that a nursing mother may awaken in anticipation of her child's cry because she and her infant dream in unison. It is suspected that the hormone, prolactin, may be the key to this mysterious link. This lasts only as long as breastfeeding is continued. With bottlefed infants and their mothers this will last only for about two weeks. After that, the mother and child have completely different and unequal sleep cycles.[30]

Research further indicates that the very deep sleep periods are extremely important and essential for restful sleep and a feeling of well-being during waking hours. When the deep sleep periods are repeatedly interrupted, the person becomes groggy, irritable, and depressed during the day.[31]

Since a mother and her nursing infant seem to have equal sleep periods, Mother also sleeps during her deep sleep periods (if no other interruptions awaken her). Should her baby awaken, this would most likely be during a lighter sleep stage. Is this, therefore, another reason why nursing mothers do not find nighttime interruptions as objectionable and are not quite as affected by them as bottlefeeding mothers? A bottlefed baby may awaken at a time when his mother is in a deep sleep period. It is no wonder that nighttime interruptions are considered a "problem" in our Western society.

An interesting and revealing study, "Sleep/Wake Patterns of Breast-fed Infants in the First Two Years of Life" (Elias et. al., 1986) reports among their findings that breastfed babies who sleep with their mothers awaken more frequently to nurse than their counterparts who do not sleep with their mothers. The co-sleeping mothers, following maternal care practices common in non-western cultures, did not, however, consider night waking a problem. It was also found that bottle-fed babies who slept by themselves slept longer hours during the night. This may seem tremendously appealing to the modern working mother. However, given the natural phenomenon of frequent nursing, touching, and the inevitable continual bonding that takes place in a co-family sleeping arrangement, one may well question the long-term effect that long, separated hours during the first few years of life may have on a child.

The "norm" for the number of hours that a "normal, healthy" baby sleeps during the night and the total number of hours he sleeps in a given day was established during the 1950's and '60's. This was at a time when most babies slept by themselves and were bottlefed. With the increase in breastfeeding and co-family sleeping, these baby book statistics will need to be changed. Breastfed babies, who are nursed and held a lot and who sleep with their mothers, require less sleep. This is a natural occurrence. As the late and well-known Dr. Shaklee urged us: "When nature speaks, we must learn to listen." (*Pediatrics* 77, 1986, pp. 322-328, "Sleep/Wake Patterns of Breastfed Infants in the First Two Years of Life," Elias et. al.).

We sometimes hear about the little baby who has his days and nights all mixed up. In talking with mothers of such babies, the circumstances are frequently the same. Baby goes to sleep for his morning nap. He is put down and sleeps for three or four hours. Then he awakens, eats, looks around a bit, and then takes another long nap. Mother is delighted with all the free time that she has while Baby is sleeping. She hesitates to pick Baby up, since he is sleeping so nicely. Then nighttime comes around. Everyone is ready for sleep—except Baby.

If Baby was carried around more during the day, however, even when dozing, he would receive enough stimulation to keep him more awake. Conseqently, he would sleep better at night.

The baby who is carried around a lot by his mother, and who takes naps in his mother's arms, is known to sleep well almost anywhere. These babies don't need a crib to nap. As long as they are close to someone, they will sleep when tired. They have learned to associate the human body with comfort, warmth, and a state of relaxation that easily lulls them to sleep when they are tired. Carrying an infant even while he is napping really doesn't deprive him of some necessary human need, which is, supposedly, to lie flat in bed while sleeping. However, this was apparently the feeling of one concerned lady upon seeing a child of eight months sleeping peacefully on his mother's lap. "That poor child," she remarked disgustedly to her friend. "He should be in his crib."

This applies to the older child as well. It really is not all that important where he sleeps, or whether he even sleeps in his pajamas, for that matter. A child will get just as much rest sleeping on the couch in his street clothes as he would in his bed in his night clothes.

Sleeping while being carried may once have been the usual way for human infants to take their naps. This still happens among peoples who take their babies wherever they go. Many readers may have seen pictures of Oriental women working in the fields, shopping at a market place, or working in a factory, with their babies strapped to their backs in a sling, peacefully sleeping.

But we do not have to cross the ocean for examples. Each year we see more and more mothers and fathers out walking, biking, or shopping with their little ones on their backs in a back carrier, or in front with a specially-designed baby sling. Frequently, these babies are fast asleep. One man even remarked: "Those carriers must be the most fantastic invention ever made. I have never yet seen a baby cry when he is carried that way. Whatever did mothers do without them?"

Babies are like adults. Some are naturally "owls," and some are naturally "larks." Some babies, no matter what their mothers do, seem to insist on being awake during the night and asleep during the day. Perhaps the most important thing to remember in a situation such as this is that *it will not last forever.*

Have a small supply of toys on hand, even for the three- to six-month-old. This can be another sleep saver for those times when the little one decides to wake up before the rest of the family wants to get up.

Many babies are most content to lie between their parents, playing, nursing, or just looking around. They might even fall asleep again for a short while.

"When will my baby sleep through the night?" This is a common question, and answered by Jane Wolfe, LLL counselor. The real issue, of course, is not "when will the *baby* sleep through the night?" but "when will *I* be able to sleep through the night?" Making this distinction is important. Certainly, an infant sleeping sixteen to twenty hours a day, more or less, is not the one who is going to be upset if he wakes up a couple of times when the sun is shining in China. The fact that you are climbing the walls in despair might cause him some concern, but as far as becoming anxious because he's not resting enough—that's no problem.

The problem is not the baby's waking up, but our getting upset about it and feeling tired because of it. We've been brainwashed by some great, tyrannical, mysterious sleep lobby (ASA—American Sleep Association, AMM—American Mattress Makers, PSPQ—Parents Seeking Peace and Quiet: these are the charter members of the sleep lobby) into thinking that, unless we have eight to nine hours of uninterrupted sleep nightly, we will be on the brink of total mental and physical collapse at the end of a few desperate days. This isn't true. Huge chunks of sleep are nice and called for occasionally, but as a steady diet they aren't necessary. Moderate-plus-small doses of sleep, and the utilization of a few conscious relaxation techniques, will do just as well (perhaps even better).

Up until Baby arrived on the scene, there was no particular need to get out from under the sleep lobby's dictates. But then he entered your life, and with his intense infant needs, calls for you with body and soul. It's four a.m. The last time you heard from him it was two a.m.

"What will it be?"

1. (a) which might not work; (b) to which he may be allergic; (c) which he certainly doesn't need; and (d) which isn't what he's calling for anyway?

2. Let him cry it out, which—(a) will exhaust him; (b) will let him get the anxious drift that when he needs you he might not be able to count on you to come; and (c) will guarantee you no sleep at all for the rest of the night?

3. (a) get up; (b) stomp into his room; (c) resentfully get him out of bed; (d) satisfy his immediate needs, but (e) basically transfer

your tension to him so that either he (1) can't get back to sleep at all; or (2) not for very long, in which case you'll be back again at five-thirty a.m.?

4. Free yourself from the terrible tyranny of the eight-to-nine-hour-a-whack sleep syndrome so that you can, with cheerful acceptance, meet your tiny one's needs at any hour, and at the same time feel happily rested and energetic?

"How to Accomplish No. 4."

1. Truly believe there is an alternative to your previous in-a-rut thinking about sleep and that this alternative is worth pursuing for the sake of you, your baby, your husband, and whoever else in your family is suffering from your present conflict (Baby's needs vs. your sleep).

2. Realize that changes in lifestyle (and this is one of them) are part of the whole business of becoming and being a mother; that they are part of the pattern of the great new personal growth that is taking place as you assume the wonderful new responsibilities that come with the birth and growth of a child. Finding new ways of rest that allow you to meet a baby's needs with enthusiasm at any hour is an exciting, not a depressing prospect.

3. Catch-up sleep, if you need it, isn't really that hard to come by. Saturdays and/or Sundays are good days for outings with Daddy.

4. Don't forget about bringing the baby to bed with you. This often serves two purposes. Baby cuddles and eats, you ZZZZZ away, and no one is the more awake for it.

5. Remember to rest when the baby rests instead of mopping and being "on the go." The early weeks, when Baby spends most of his time asleep, is the best time for learning the art of smaller-chunk sleeping. Try resting when Baby does. If you don't get to sleep every time, at least you'll be learning to relax, and probably will sleep some of the time.

According to Luce and Segal, co-authors of the two books *Sleep* and *Insomnia*, many people get more sleep than they think they do. It is evidently difficult to estimate how much sleep one is actually getting. Unless one can see his EEG tracings, say Luce and Segal, he doesn't really know for sure. But the lack of sleep is most likely overestimated. One may have dozed off half a dozen times without knowing it. It should be of some satisfaction to know, however, that the discomfort due to lack of sleep is seldom as disastrous as one may think.[32] It is usually self-pity which stands in the way of feeling o.k. about whatever amount of sleep one gets.

A mother may strive to have her little one sleep through the night, but there is little she can do to attain this goal. Through-the-night sleeping appears to require a certain maturation of the brain. It is not a matter of love, nor of the baby's intelligence. Sleep is not a skill to be learned, and the baby will progress at his own rate of development.[33]

Studies also show that giving solids to a baby has little or no effect on the child's sleeping through the night. Some babies begin sleeping through the night at seven days old. Others are four years old before they sleep through in one stretch. Some babies, after sleeping continually during the night for several months or even years, may suddenly begin to awaken at night. They may wake up once or twice for several days or months before sleeping through the night again. Frequently we do not know what causes the change. But this we do know: if they call us, they need us.

Most nursing mothers find lying down with an infant to be very relaxing. With a first baby, it might take a few trials before finding the most comfortable position, but this usually does not take long at all. It is important to remember that whichever position you and your baby find most comfortable is the one best for both of you.

La Leche League's manual, *The Womanly Art of Breastfeeding*, gives this suggestion when first lying down with your baby:

> If you are going to nurse your baby on the right side, lie down on that side, put your right arm up over the baby's head or under it, whichever is more comfortable for you. With the left arm, bring the baby toward you *till his cheek is touching your breast*, with the nipple next to his mouth. He will turn his head toward it, for this is the way he is built, and open his mouth. When he does, pull him a bit closer, just enough so he can get the nipple into his mouth and suck. For nursing on the left side, reverse all this. If you pull his legs close to you, it angles his body enough to keep his nose free. This keeps him warm and cozy besides.[34]

When ready to nurse Baby on the other side, gently pull him close against your body, roll over, and settle down on the other side. You can also do this while he is still nursing.

It might be comfortable in the beginning to tuck a pillow behind your back. Once you become really adept at nursing lying down, you could try "overlapping." This refers to nursing the baby with the left breast, but remaining on your right side. It is not quite as comfortable, but it can be very convenient.

It is always our intention to provide as safe an environment as possible for our children. Nevertheless, dangers lurk everywhere. The following letter was taken from the La Leche League publication, *Leaven,* in November of 1974.

> I have appreciated the recent warning about how little ones can swallow pins, zipper pulls, etc., but thought, "I'm careful, that will never happen to me." One never can tell . . . Last night around 3:00 a.m. I brought the baby into bed with us to nurse, unbuttoned my pretty nightie and untied the shoestring bow at the top, put her to the breast and promptly fell back to sleep. When I awoke this morning and rolled over, I noticed the tie was caught and pulled gently to free it. When it wouldn't come loose I looked to see what it was caught on and was horrified to see it was wrapped twice around the baby's neck, loosely but nonetheless firm. I gently freed it and as I hugged Sarah close to me shuddered to think what combinations of her movements or mine might have produced a tragedy. As I cut the bow off the nightie this morning I thought how many other mothers might have nighties with long bows or shoestring ties. I know I have another gown that is perfect for nursing, for it ties over each shoulder, but, when undone, those ties are about twelve inches long and equally as dangerous as last night's nightdress.
>
> I am surprised I didn't consider the danger of those ties, for I did think of the danger of the venetian blind cord (actually a perfect hangman's loop) on the window near her bed, and had taken great care to hook it up where Sarah couldn't reach it. Ceiling-to-floor curtain cords also present a similar danger to creepers.

Because our beds are usually too small and too high, and the bedroom too crowded with the regular bedroom furniture, most families who turn to family sleeping have had to improvise in making accommodations for the whole family to sleep together. A mother wrote: "When Baby gets big enough to roll out of bed we have to push furniture against the open end as a safety measure. Some interior decorators would cringe. I have had guests who think it is an awful way to sleep and live. Their criticism falls on deaf ears. In a few short years all the children will be grown and gone and we can have a wall-to-wall Better Homes and Gardens bedroom then."

Some parents have been fortunate enough to be able to buy a larger bed, or have resorted to placing two twin-sized beds together. One father wrote his solution in an amusing poem.

Father's Lib (at 2:00 a.m.)

Oh, how nice it would be,
If other Dads could be like me.
While they're up and bottles pouring,
I'm in bed soundly snoring!
—That is, of course, if there is room.

At 1 a.m. Baby pops in,
Then a toddler kicks me in the shin.
Mommy's hanging off the edge,
Sister's on the other ledge.
Poor Dad can't move or do a thing—
Except to buy a SUPER KING![35]

Wally Bennett

Pillows and blankets or foam rubber pads around a low bed have served as safety measures until the baby could crawl from the bed by himself. Some parents have even resorted to the most logical solution — a wall-to-wall bed made just from mattresses.

But, as logical as it might seem, it may not always be the most practical, or even necessary. To enlarge the parents' bed, an adjustable crib can be placed right next to the big bed, set to the height of the bed. Or a picnic bench can be placed between the bed and the wall, built up with blankets to the height of the master bed. The slight space between can be covered with a blanket or bed pad. Two chairs, facing each other, with a board bridging the seats, will also solve the problem.

If there is enough room, another bed can be placed in the parents' room, either next to their bed, on the foot end, or somewhere else in the room. A side rail is another solution. Or placing the bed in a corner against the wall, and having the children sleep between Mom and the wall. A mattress or sleeping bag on the floor next to the big bed has also been a good solution. (Watch out for drafts, though.)

One mother wrote, "My husband built a sleeping platform for us. It is seven feet long and eight feet wide, and two inches off the floor. The size was deliberately planned for three, since we realized that neither Baby nor ourselves would welcome a separation. Baby has been with us all this time. We took her crib down after a few months and have resolved never to use it again."

The urine, bowel movement, or vomit of a totally breastfed baby does not have an unpleasant smell. Should the baby or young child wet the bed, a towel placed under him will quickly give him a dry place to sleep again. Keep a towel handy under your pillow for such emergencies. A rubberized flannel sheet beneath the bedsheet prevents the mattress from getting wet. Putting a double diaper on Baby will also help prevent wet sheets.

For naps, the infant may be safest in that time-honored little bed, the cradle. It is a snug and secure place, perfect for lulling the baby to sleep. The gentle back and forth motion of the cradle simulates the mother's movements and walking. A buggy in the living room will serve the same purpose.

If a problem arises for which no immediate solution can be found or which seems momentarily irritating, it is important not to think, "If he had been in his own bed..." because this leads to resentment. Rather, accept the fact that he sleeps in your bed, and find a solution, not a cop-out.

Unfortunately, ours is a society in which we are conditioned to find instant solutions to unpleasant situations. Instant weight-reduction foods, pills, menus, and gadgets are big sellers these days. (It says so on the package!) We can buy instant meals—from breakfast to frozen dinners. We have instant pain relievers. "Instant Possession, Pay Later," blare the advertisements. Babysitters and separate bedrooms instantly relieve us of our children.

When we are faced with a problem concerning our children for which there is no instant solution, then we panic. We are pressured into finding an immediate answer, instead of receiving encouragement, understanding, and support for what we are going through and doing to make the best of the situation.

"Only as we discover and assimilate the truth about nature," wrote Lorenz, "shall we be able to undertake the apparently contradictory but essential task of reestablishing our unity with nature and at the same time maintaining our transcendence over nature."[36]

Society has moved the infant away from his mother at a time when, in normal cases, separation is totally contraindicated. Mother and Baby need each other, and every effort should be made to meet this natural necessity. Nature is not perfect. And we can benefit from the learnings of men. However, man must not find himself so confident that he chooses to ignore the natural emotions of the new couple. These emotions must be respected and protected, for only then can a mother and her child grow.

9

The Child Past Infancy

The child's sob in the silence curses deeper
Than the strong man in his wrath.

Elizabeth B. Browning
"The cry of the children"

There is almost unanimous agreement that it is not unusual for the young child to feel lonesome or frightened at night. Parents are advised, therefore, to leave a light on in the child's room or in the hallway, and to be sure he has his favorite blanket or toy.

"But the real reason for his loneliness," contends Montagu, "the primary need for the child to have close and warm contact with another person's body, is totally disregarded."[1]

Children, however, are rather adaptable creatures. Placed in single beds or isolated in separate bedrooms, they will snuggle up to their toys.[2] Dolls are now available that talk to the child, similar to the way he would like his mommy to talk to him. Parents are urged to buy the doll, which is advertised as follows:

> When you're two and a half and you've just been tucked into bed, don't you wish that falling asleep weren't so lonesome? That's what this doll is for. It's so nice when someone stays with you to keep you company until you fall asleep. And you couldn't hope to find a softer sleepmate than this doll. It lulls you to sleep with phrases like, "Mommy, kiss me goodnight." "Mommy, hug me tight." "Mommy, I love you."

Owing to the misconception that it is healthy for children to sleep, rest, and play alone, children are forced to sleep by themselves instead of in the parental bed. "This neglect of natural needs," says Anna Freud, "is the first break in the smooth functioning of the processes of need and drive fulfillment." As a result, mothers seek advice for children with sleep difficulties.

Montagu describes these difficulties well: "In our Western culture, one constantly encounters the phenomenon of children begging their mothers to lie by their sides or at least to stay with them until they fall asleep." But mothers tend to discourage these requests. The child's endless cries for his mother, an open door, a drink of water, a light, a story, to be tucked in, and so on—all are symptoms that Montagu regards as the child's need for that primary object, his mother, to whom he can securely relate. When Mother's presence is lacking, the child resorts to other means of falling asleep. A cuddly toy, a pet one can take to bed, soft materials, and autoerotic activities (such as thumb-sucking, rocking, and masturbation) are means to which the child may resort in his drive for security. "When these objects are given up," continues Montagu, "a new wave of difficulties in falling asleep may develop."[3] Granted, the child should not be denied a doll or teddy bear in bed with him, but he should also have his Mama or Papa, at least until he is sound asleep.

Children may still ask for water, a story, or one more bathroom visit. Perhaps the child is not tired enough and is therefore bored with being in bed even though a parent is with him. Keep a glass of water by the bed regularly. It's unjust to deny water to a thirsty child. Thirst is a very uncomfortable feeling. But if one of my children did indeed drink some water, I would make sure I picked her up and put her on the toilet a few hours after she had gone to sleep. I did this quite frequently when my children were small. Such a procedure never awakened them enough to cause difficulty in their falling asleep again. I would either carry her to the bathroom or help her to her feet and guide her, using Edwina Froehlich's method and simply telling her, "Walk." It works. A story before sleep is a favorite bedroom ritual of children and adults alike. Besides that, it's a treasured time of relaxed closeness, a time so rare in our culture.

What about the time that one spends lying down with his children until they have fallen asleep? This may sometimes take as long as an hour. Is this time being wasted? We can readily think of a million things we could be doing. Is there anything to be gained? Yes, there is. For the child, it means a happy, secure feeling of love and a relaxing way to fall asleep. For the parent, it means a chance for growth, maturing in the ability to freely give himself to those who need him, to place his immediate wants and needs second to someone else's wants and needs. This is one of the most noble acts in life.

If it takes much longer for the child to fall asleep, he may be overstimulated and may not have had a chance to relax. Or he may not have had enough play and fresh air and sun during the day. Mothers with busy schedules, air-conditioned houses in the summer, and a fear of catching a cold in the winter, sometimes forget the importance of outdoor play for a child.

And don't forget the weather. It can have forceful influences on people, and has a lot to do with the way a person acts and feels. Although children may not seem to be bothered as much as adults by extremes of temperature and humidity, these conditions, nevertheless, may affect their ability to fall asleep. Also, the barometric pressure has an influence on the way we behave and feel.[4] Ask a teacher. He will tell you when a storm is on its way!

Difficulty in falling asleep may be due to a long, late nap. Even a short nap late in the afternoon may refresh a child so much that he is not sleepy at bedtime.

Individual children differ in their need for sleep by as much as two to three hours. Watch for the signs that indicate when he is ready for bed, advises Newton. Fussing and irritability, whining, quarreling, and bumping into things more than usual may be signs of fatigue.[5]

It is important for the child to know what is expected of him at bedtime. And it helps when he can count on some kind of a ritual. Choose whatever seems most pleasant and relaxing: a short walk, a bath, reading a story, a snack.

Having a calm time prior to bedtime is generally accepted as wise advice. In a pediatric textbook of the 1850's, however, it was said that children should run around for half an hour before bedtime. This would then insure a good night's sleep.

Diet could have an influence on a person's sleeping behavior. With all the prepared and refined foods on the shelves these days, it is easy for children to fill up on junk food rather than a wholesome diet. The child may, therefore, be deficient in one or more essential nutrients. Irritability or excitability may also be caused by an allergic reaction to food or food additives. Just try taking a child off sugar for three weeks and you will be amazed at the results. An absolute angel can be transformed into a little devil when sugar gets into his system. It's a real mood alternator.

The unfortunate thing is that, even though the child can't help being "bad" when he has a reaction to food or food additives, he is still the recipient of our frustration. And that isn't fair—not to mention the tremendous negative emotional impact our anger has on the child. As a matter of fact, you might try taking the whole family off junk food and see what happens. Then you can go one step further. Start supplementing the family diet with natural foods, vitamins, and minerals.

Numerous books on the subject of nutrition are now available at health food stores. A consultation with a doctor of natural or preventive medicine may also be well worthwhile.

Experiments by psychologists show that we remember, through our sleep, the words spoken at bedtime. Newton, therefore, warns us never to make bedtime a punishment. This does not mean, of course, that discipline should not be used when necessary. But once the child has been sent to bed as a disciplinary measure, he may well associate it with unpleasantness, and naturally put up more resistance.[6]

The child may not want to go to sleep if he has not had enough love and attention from his parents. Bedtime can thus be a good opportunity to spend some relaxing moments with the child. Make him feel that, for a little while, he can have full possession of his parents' time. Doing this in short sessions during the day may also help considerably.

One mother wrote me of the following experiences she has had with bedtime rituals with her children.

> When my four-year-old daughter (she is fifteen now) napped, it was often in our bed. I would lie down with her and usually read a story. One afternoon, as we were getting ready to nap, she asked, "Can we have a little talk first?" Somehow I never forgot this and have often thought that, just as conversation and relaxation are an enjoyable part of sharing the bed for parents, so it must also be for children. When I think of it we always precede our sleep, nighttime or naptime, with a little talk, whether the children are sleeping with us or in their own beds.
>
> Lately, our present four-year-old has been talking a lot before going to sleep. He talks primarily with his Daddy. This serves a good purpose because Daddy doesn't get a chance to hear him well until the rest of the noisy brothers and sisters are out of the way. The child's stories amuse my husband and it relaxes him so his mood is more restful for the remainder of the evening. Maybe a lot of other Daddies could unwind in this way and respond to the needs of their children at the same time.

I just asked my fifteen-year-old daughter if she remembered the incident I referred to in the first paragraph. She said she did, although she may have cheated a bit by reading her baby book, since it is among the cherished things I've recorded. Maintaining good relations with a teenage daughter isn't easy. I'm grateful for whatever communication we established during her first five years of life, even when it involved giving up my sleep, marital privacy, and all the heated discussions on child rearing with my contemporaries in which I was always the underdog. I'm still the minority report at bridge games and coffee parties. But the role isn't uncomfortable because we've experienced a measure of success while putting our ideas to work.

For several months when our older daughter was five years old, she asked both my husband and me to lie by her, one on each side, until she fell asleep. She would put an arm on each of us, give us a hug, and say, "I'm going to sleep with my Mama and Papa right next to me. Goodnight!"

Sometimes, instead of reading a book or talking, I was asked, "Tell me about when you were a little girl." I encourage parents to tell their children stories from their own childhood. If you want to give your children a real legacy, put the stories down in writing for them. They will love it.

Bedtime can be smooth. It might take several years and several children to learn this fact, but it *is* possible. So even when you falter along the way, take a deep breath and try again. It's worth it.

The following letter was taken from the *La Leche League News* of May, 1974. Mothers may smile as I did when reading it. Aside from its humor, it rings a bell with respect to the questions, answers, and emotions at bedtime with a little child.

I had saved putting him to bed until last because he is the hardest. Michael Patrick ... three years old. His daddy and I call him the blond bombshell. His five brothers and sisters have all been individually Bible-lessoned, storied, prayered, watered, and tucked in. Michael is sitting on his bed, impatiently waiting for me to lie down with him. I look over to where his adopted brother, four months younger, is already asleep; curled into a little brown ball. Raised in a foster home for twenty months, he has always gone to sleep like a model child. I'm tired from a busy day; all I want is a leisurely bath and to go to bed early. Michael is urging me to "hurry up and lie down with me" and I wonder where I went wrong. Why won't this child go to bed by himself?

Michael wants a song. But it's not that simple. He wants me to play my guitar and sing. Two choruses of "I've Been Working on the Railroad." Later, I carefully and logically explain that Mommy wants to take a bath and caution Michael that he is to stay in bed until Mommy finishes and then I'll lie down with him again. Blue eyes regard me solemnly and blond hair bobs as he nods his consent, but as I walk out the door he warns me, "A fast bath!"

The water is running into the tub and I'm pinning my hair up when I hear the familiar pitter-patter of hurried footsteps down the hall to my bedroom, a satisfied "thump" and I know he's in my bed. I take a hurried bath (is there any other kind?), dress, retrieve Michael from my bed, and we start all over again.

"I thought you promised Mommy to stay in your bed until I finished my bath?"

"I did, Mommy. But then when you were gone, I got a'scared and zoomed to your room."

Pretty soon we're both tucked into Michael's single bed. Very cozy. Nurtured on the closeness of the nursing relationship, Michael is a toucher. His arms are wrapped around my neck, his legs plopped across mine, his silky blond hair snuggled against my cheek. I savor the moment, but also wish he'd hurry and go to sleep. I have things to do and I'm tired.

The silence lasts but a minute. "Mommy . . . your teeth look pretty and clean."

"Thank you, Michael. I just brushed them."

"Mommy . . . why does teeth get dirty?"

"Because food gets on them." Silence again. Then, "Mommy . . . how does water get off your toothbrush after you put it away in the cupboard?" Mentally I discard the word "evaporation" and answer, "Because the air moves around it inside the cupboard and dries it off." Silence again.

"Mommy . . . how did God make the first man?" I explain the story of Creation, how the first man was formed from the dust of the earth, how God breathed life into him and he became a living creature. Impish giggles! "Was his name Raymond Sheron?" (Daddy's name) "No, Michael, you know better than that. His name was Adam."

"I know the lady's name. Her name was Even." I suppress a chuckle. "Well, almost. Her name was Eve. She was a beautiful lady."

"Mommy . . . how was I made?"

Oh, wow! I'm tired, half asleep, and I've got the story of reproduction ahead of me. Patiently and filled with the wonder and miracle of it myself, I carefully explain how Michael grew safe and warm inside of me until he was big enough and ready to be born.

"How did I get out of you?" I explain that he was born through a special opening made especially for that purpose. Silence for a moment, then, "Where is the opening?" I explain. More silence. I wonder what he's going to ask next.

"Mommy . . . why don't pigs have hair?" My mind boggles at the sudden change in subject. "Well," I begin gamely, "if pigs had hair like you and me, when they wallowed in the mud, it would get all stuck in their hair and make them messy." Thankfully he's satisfied with my improvised answer.

"Why did Mrs. Centers cut up her pig?" Long ago he spent the day with a friend the day they butchered their hog. I explained that they needed it for food.

"We don't do that, do we? We get our food from the store." We are vegetarians so the idea of killing animals for food was new to him. He seemed a little disturbed by it.

He turns over and snuggles down into his covers. I think the magic moment has arrived, but not yet. "Mommy . . ." And I am entertained with a long and complicated adventure story plucked from the world of "pretend" involving himself and his imaginary horse Trigger. As he talks his eyes get rounder and rounder and his eyebrows disappear under his long, blond bangs as his face becomes more animated. Finally the story is over, he begins to yawn. He turns toward me again, takes my hand in both of his and is almost instantly asleep.

Suddenly I am caught up by those feelings of tenderness and over-whelming good will that a sleeping child bestows. There is something about sleep that transforms children into angels. Tangled lashes lie against cheeks still soft and round with a hint of babyhood still lingering. I gently kiss the soft mouth that in infancy searched eagerly for my breast and the milk that was his sole nourishment for the first six months. At almost two years that same mouth was known on many inopportune occasions to demand, "I want to nurse." Usually in church or the supermarket. And then one day to sit up from nursing and lament, "I don't like it." And he was weaned.

As I slip quietly from bed, I am suddenly aware of the instinct of children to demand what they need. Busy with five other children and a full day, were it not for his terrible bedtime habits, I might not have found time for this special hour with Michael, for cuddling and just learning to know him. I thank God that he was born healthy, and bright, and whole, and even the knowledge that he'll probably be back in our bed before midnight can't destroy the peace that I feel at this moment.

Why are children afraid of the dark? Kenny and Schreiter's explana-tion makes it very clear:

Fear of the dark is very prevalent in childhood, from age two months
to almost age eight. Darkness shrouds the normal visual and depth-per-
ception cues that give the child his orientation within the environment.
Not only do cues for the environment vanish, but even the child's own
body vanishes, making him as invisible as the rest of the world. This
situation produces anxiety. The child is left with only sounds and touch.
But severing the visual from the auditory sense, sight from hearing,
causes a great deal of anxiety. It seems that during light hours the child
attends more to sight than to hearing; he understands sound stimuli
only in reference to a seen object. Hence in the dark he has trouble
connecting noises with their visual source. With the world of sight
gone, the child is left with the world of sounds—the world of the wind,
animal noises, and sirens—a world he could not attend to during the
day. To make matters worse, the child is often "privileged" with his
own room and confined in his own bed. This means no older person
is there to reassure or protect him against the things that go "bump"
in the night. But even the presence of another person in the room may
not be enough. Usually children end up by scurrying into bed with the
other person. Why? When darkness has taken sight, when sound is
threatening, then touch is all that is left. It is a return to a period when
things were not so threatening, when being curled up in the womb was
a way of life. The child will move in with whoever is close—preferably
the parents, although an older brother or sister will do.[7]

According to Bowlby, blind children are evidently more afraid of
such common fear-arousing situations as mechanical noises, thunder,
and wind. The principle reason, he feels, is that their contact with
the world depends greatly on touch. When out of contact with their
attachment figure, usually their mother, they may experience more
intense fright.[8]

The very young child does not have a past experience upon which
to rely. To him, if something is out of sight, it does not exist any more.
Mothers know from experience that their very young children go
through a stage of crying frantically when they leave the room momentarily. Even Mother's voice, calling from another room, is not enough
to calm her child. Most children go through this stage. Should the
child awaken at night, he experiences these same fears of having lost
his mother.

As the child grows older, he is less likely to be upset by separation.
It is easier for him to understand that his mother will return. His
nighttime fears are no longer based primarily on fear of separation, as

is the case of the younger child, but on fears aroused by his imagination, or other forms of anxiety. Indeed, fear of the dark and of being alone is a feeling that most of us never quite master completely.[9]

According to Luce and Segal, falling asleep is probably a more intense experience for children and adolescents than for mature people. The brain of a child is developing rapidly; it will triple in size from birth to age six. The nervous system is learning everything from bodily control to speech and other complicated skills, such as control over feelings. "With this internal ferment of growing," write Luce and Segal, "a child lies down to rest and he feels a variety of sensations. As a person drifts down into sleep, the brain is changing its functions. Certain brain cells seem to let go of their controls spasmodically. The result is a sudden convulsive jerk of the body. The half-asleep person may think he is falling, and wake up with a start. To a child, the sensation of falling may be both real and frightening. And this is just one of the sharp and unfamiliar sensations that come from the normal activity going on within the child's body and brain."[10]

Falling asleep may be especially frightening to the child who is alone in his room. He may resist going to bed because he vaguely remembers this fear, yet he is unable to explain it to an adult. It would be ridiculous to tell him, "there is nothing to be afraid of," if he is experiencing fright. Fear is a real feeling, and should not be lightly dismissed or ridiculed.

Fear at bedtime may be aroused by a parent's innocent remarks. One mother used to say to her son, "Goodnight, and don't let the bedbugs bite." To the utter perplexity of his parents, this boy used to wake up screaming that there were bugs in his bedroom. His father would then go into the room and "kill" all the bugs. After that the boy went off to sleep again. Nonetheless, it was a most disturbing experience for everyone. His behavior remained a mystery until a friend overheard the boy's mother repeat her goodnight blessing.

Some children may come to fear sleep or have fears while going to sleep because of the possibility of death as expressed in some bedtime prayers.[11]

> Now I lay me down to sleep
> I pray the Lord my soul to keep.
> If I should die before I wake,
> I pray the Lord my soul to take.

Some books on child rearing warn Mother not to allow children to sleep with her, even when Dad is away on a trip, lest the children begin to look forward to seeing Daddy off. If this is the only time that the children get to enter the family bed, the advice might indeed be justified. But when I mentioned this to mothers whose children sleep on and off in the family bed, all were taken aback and exclaimed, "But this is not true. Nothing will take the place of Daddy!"

When parents have decided to change from letting the child have his own bed to allowing him in bed with his siblings or with them, they should realize that things may not go all that smoothly at first. The child may not really know or understand how to handle the fun of sleeping with someone else, which he probably only associates with rough-housing and games. It may take several nights before he becomes accustomed to sleeping with others.

With my own child, Yvonne, who did not join us until she was almost two and a half years old, I found that it was an endless struggle to ask her to lie still and be quiet. So I finally decided to let her wiggle and talk, within reason, and I found that after a while she would fall asleep anyway. Her sleep came no later than if I had repeatedly asked her to remain quiet and still. And there was no nagging or tension. As she became older, she quieted down considerably.

What do you do when you have dinner guests, and your youngsters, who have to go to bed, are used to having you with them while they fall asleep? We only have dinner or after-dinner guests when my husband is home. When the children are ready for bed, I make sure that the adults have enough to eat and drink, and I quietly disappear. As soon as the youngsters are asleep I return. Actually, after the hustle and bustle of trying to get the house cleaned up, cooking dinner, setting the table—in the meantime, keeping children away from the stove, the waste paper basket, and the table, plus getting them ready for bed—it is quite refreshing to be able to lie down for a little while. Guests and friends are important and fun to have over. (It's also exciting for the children. All the more reason not to send them away from the party to go to sleep by themselves!) But the ultimate happiness of one's children should come first. With a little forethought and explanation, things can usually be worked out to the satisfaction of all concerned. Wait just a little while past the children's regular bedtime before putting them to bed, so you may be gone no more than a short while.

After a certain age, some children may not *want* to join the family bed. Some loving talk and attention, and a friendly backrub at bedtime, may be a good way to end the day for these children. Dr. Riordan, a La Leche League Medical Advisor, suggests that such a backrub at bedtime is often the most effective and least expensive psychological therapy on days when things haven't gone smoothly between parent and child. (*LLL News*, Sept. '70) He further states that, by rubbing the child's back, the parent shows he still cares for the youngster, and the child is reassured that he's not undesirable.

Occasionally we hear of the older baby who is used to sleeping in his own crib and simply *refuses* to sleep in his parents' bed. He wiggles and struggles and cries and screams. As soon as he's put in his crib, he quiets down and goes to sleep, perhaps with a favorite toy or blanket. The parents feel rejected and resentful because the baby prefers his crib and blanket to them. They may feel that he is disowning them.

While this entire book attempts to explain why parents should not struggle to keep children *out* of the parental bed, it is ironic that we should have to discuss the case of parents who struggle to keep them *in* the family bed.

There is no simple solution to this problem, mainly because there may be factors involved that we do not know, but which make a baby act in this manner. The most important thing to remember is that love does persevere and conquer all. He will outgrow his crib and blanket, but he will always have his parents' love. Perhaps the child would be content to sleep with his parents if he was allowed to keep his blanket with him; or perhaps the crib could be taken down, and Baby could sleep on a mattress in a corner of his or their room. The parent might lie next to the child to give him a sense of human closeness as he falls asleep.

Relax and realize that little babies are individuals, also, with individual wants and needs that must be respected. All we can do is be patient and, above all else, love. *Relax* and *love*.

The parent of a child who is ill, unless very ill, will benefit greatly from having the family accustomed to sleeping together. Many a wakeful night of floor-walking has been averted because a feverish, unhappy child has been able to snuggle up to his parents and, if he were still breastfeeding, nurse himself off to sleep. More so than a healthy child, a child who does *not* feel well seeks and needs the presence of his mother. And many mothers have expressed the good feeling of being close at hand when a child has become ill at night. It has also given parents a sense of comfort to know that they were always aware of the child's well-being. One mother writes, "Our middle child has bronchial complications with about every cold. We all feel better having her sleep with us during the nights when breathing is a chore for her. I'm able to keep her propped up on a pillow between us, and she sleeps better knowing that we're next to her."

For the Mom who does not feel well herself, this means being able to remain in bed, usually without even having to sit up, should one of the children or the baby need attention. When one is tired or ill, such a horizontal position is like a little bit of heaven.

Our society tends to ignore a child's need for the presence of another person at night. Enforced loneliness is greatly encouraged, even when he is not ready to be separated. Many children, through nature's wise efforts, make attempts to counter this unnatural situation. But the taboo against co-family sleeping is so strong that every effort is made to find material substitutes with which the child is supposed to be content, happy, and satisfied. But what could ever take the place of a real person!

10

Siblings

Experience is the child of Thought, and
Thought is the child of Action.

Benjamin Disraeli

"Sometimes I do, sometimes I don't," announces four-year-old Amy, as she tells her mother that tonight she wants to sleep with her older sister, instead of in her parents' bed. And this is how weaning from the parental bed begins — gradually, at the child's own pace. It can be so gradual that some parents have a difficult time remembering just when it happened.

The age at which this takes place depends entirely on the individual child. It also depends on whether he has another sibling with whom he can sleep, and whether he has slept in his parents' bed from birth on.

It seems that, after a certain age, the emotionally-stable child no longer needs the direct, touching security of his parents, but will be content to sleep away from them as long as he can sleep with another person.

Parents find that those children who had their own bed from birth on, but were allowed to visit the parental bed occasionally, tend to keep returning to the family bed much longer than those children who slept with their parents from birth on. The fear, write parents, that this will become an unbreakable habit, has not been substantiated in such cases.

In one family, the graduation took place one night when the five-year-old, after some restless moving around in the "big bed," sat up and looked around. After a few moments, she exclaimed, "It sure is crowded in here," took her pillow, and went to sleep in her own bed.

Many parents feel that having siblings sleep together results in a more peaceful home. "Among other things," wrote a parent, "we've found that when two children sleep together they get along better the next day. We feel it's fostering a closer relationship between them, and nightmares and other nighttime disturbances are really rare."

Another mother said, "I have two children who fought a great deal and did not like to sleep with anyone. Due to necessity, at ages five and six these two children had to start sharing the same bed. They began to get along much better. They didn't even mind snuggling with each other after a while. I later found out that my brother had this same experience with his two daughters. At ages six and seven, they needed to sleep together to make room for another baby. He remarked how much better the two girls had gotten along since they began to sleep together."

Some families play musical beds. "My children sleep with whomever they feel like. It makes for a happy situation. They especially like to take turns sleeping with the baby (the youngest) of the family," wrote a mother.

Is sibling rivalry normal? Dr. Lee Salk answers that, since it is common in our Western world, it is statistically normal. He feels that it is a struggle for recognition and attention.[1] Our society has not made it easy for children. Usually, grandparents, aunts, and uncles do not live with or close to the young family. These relatives cannot share in the love and attention that young ones need on a daily basis. Studies of anthropologists prove that, in groups in which the extended family lives with or near the nuclear family, and in which not one but many adults take responsibility for the children, sibling rivalry exists very little or not at all.

But most of us don't have other adults living with us. Some mothers find themselves faced with the problem of how to pay equal attention to all children. The parent must simply take command of the situation and decide how the children are going to take turns being close to her, both in bed and out of it. Remember, this is not going to last. For six weeks after our second child was born, I never sat down but always had two children on my lap—my baby and my two-year-old. Then, quite abruptly one day, the older one slipped off and that was the end of my constant companion. She had her need fulfilled.

Some nursing children are perfectly happy to sleep with older siblings when Mom is not around to nurse them off to sleep. "When my husband and I are out for the evening," wrote a breastfeeding mother, "my thirteen-month-old baby is content to go to sleep with one of his brothers or his sister."

A parent of six children offered several reasons why her family sleeps together.

1. Nobody is afraid of noises, thunder, lightning, or being alone in a dark room.
2. Body warmth helps them to sleep soundly—especially the smaller children, who become uncovered so easily.
3. They are learning to share sleeping quarters, which is something they will have to do later on when they go camping, and then when they get married. Not one of my children has ever demanded "his own bed" or "his own room." This could be due also to the fact that my husband and I share the family bed, and the children think this is the only way to sleep.
4. The youngest child feels cared for and the older ones learn to take care of the needs of their younger siblings, such as bringing them a glass of water—many of the things that Mother would have to do during the course of the evening or the night.

Another question of concern to the newcomer to co-family sleeping is whether there is the possibility that older siblings of the opposite sex will engage in sexual activity. When should boy and girl be put into separate beds or bedrooms? This depends on the family situation. Did the children sleep with their parents? Did they sleep together when they were young? Is the family closeknit, where the need for love and touching has been fulfilled? When a girl starts to mature sexually, she usually becomes very modest and will most likely ask for her own bed or room. If siblings were intent on having sex, they would do so in extreme secrecy. They might be exhibiting fulfillment of a need that was not satisfied during early childhood. A number of parents indicated their family slept together until, one by one, the children left for college.

One woman wrote that she slept with her brother, two years older than she, until he went off to college. She never thought anything of it until she went to college herself to study psychiatry. She then found out how "potentially dangerous and abnormal" it was for siblings to sleep together. For years she felt guilty because she never gave co-family sleeping a second thought, until she "discovered" that she was really emotionally quite stable and happy.

Sleeping together calls for sharing and a consideration of others. When children have the chance to learn this within the family unit, it strengthens them as individuals, as members of the family, and the family as a whole becomes stronger.

When a child no longer needs the particular presence of his parents, he will frequently choose to sleep with and find comfort in being with his brothers and sisters. One mother suggested that a pet, such as a dog or cat, may provide a good sibling substitute for the only child who has outgrown the family bed.

Our present-day society is aimed at educating and rearing the child as a strong, independent individual. He has his own activities, his own playthings, his own schedules, and sometimes even his own meal-times. He is part of and yet alone in his position in his family. Sleeping together is thus a logical way to end the day and keep each child in touch with the other members of the family. Much can be said for the children of a family who enjoy each other's presence and find comfort in it.

11

Marital Relations

Kindness in words creates confidence.
Kindness in thinking creates profoundness.
Kindness in giving creates love.

It comes as no surprise that one of the first questions concerning children in the parental bed is, "But what about one's sex life?"

Our country is predominantly sex-oriented. The breasts are associated with sex instead of as a source of life for a newborn infant. The bed is frequently associated with "going to bed with someone" or "having sex with someone." We can gauge our sex life by comparing it with charts that tell us exactly how much is "normal." Article after article is printed in popular publications on the subject of sex. Countless people even believe, write Luce and Segal, that sex is essential to a good night's sleep.

The fact that children sleep with their parents is considered by many people to be highly indecent and immoral. Yet, in spite of society's preoccupation with separate beds and bedrooms, supposedly to "guard" children and give them a moral upbringing, sexual promiscuity among teenagers and adults knows almost no limits, even though premarital or extra-marital sexual relations are greatly taboo.

This strong interest in sex may be an indirect result of the minimal physical contact that much of the younger generation has received during infancy. Perhaps some inner drive is attempting to repair the damage of too little bodily stimulation during childhood.

In a cross-cultural study on child rearing practices, compiled by Dr. James W. Prescott, it was pointed out that there seems to be a direct correlation between the amount of body pleasure during infancy, the practice of premarital sexual behavior, and adult interpersonal relations. In most of the societies studied, the following pattern was observed: minimal holding, caressing, and fondling of infants would in most cases result in violent adult interpersonal behavior patterns, unless premarital sexual relations were socially accepted and tolerated. Conversely, those societies that gave a great deal of physical attention to the infant were characterized by minimal adult interpersonal violence.[1]

Anthropological accounts report a correlation between the violence exhibited by a people in their everyday living (i.e., disharmony among members of a family or tribe, active warring, torturing of the enemy, violent or painful initiation rites) and their interest in sex. Namely, sexual drives seemed to be stronger in violent people than among people who were peaceful, lived harmoniously, and whose total image revealed gentleness. Dr. Prescott concludes his report by saying that he feels interpersonal violence in human societies can be minimized by maximizing physical affection during infancy, childhood, and adolescence.[2] Likewise, Janov expresses the opinion that a loved child does not grow up into an adult with an insatiable craving for sex. The child, says Janov, has been held and caressed by his parents and does not need to use sex to satisfy that early need.[3]

Adults' possessive interest in sex and the inability to tolerate interferences—one of these being children in the parental bed—may thus be a manifestation of unfulfilled sensory stimulation during infancy.

One mother wrote, "I feel that, by keeping children in the parental bed a little bit longer, perhaps they will stay out of a premarital bed a bit longer. Maybe some of those adolescent kids who crawl into bed with each other are really looking for Mama, except Mama was never there."

The taboos that society places upon sexual matters are not the result of biological heredity; rather, they are the result of cultural training.[4] Although in our society it is strongly believed that when children observe sexual relations, such observations may lead to neuroses later in the child's life, other societies hold quite different views. Newton adds that if observation of the primal act is really as upsetting as some psychoanalysts maintain, large numbers of historical and traditional peoples would have been neurotic.[5]

There are, indeed, cultures other than Western society in which great pains are taken to avoid children's observation and indulgence in sex. However, adult neurosis has not been mentioned as the reason for such avoidance.

On the other hand, there are societies in which sex is an encouraged subject. Children are allowed to observe sexual behavior and to participate in the discussion of sexual matters. The older children of the Chewaos in Africa build little huts some distance from the village, and with complete approval of the parents, play at being husband and wife. It is believed by this tribe that, unless children begin to exercise themselves sexually early in life, they will never have children.[6] Between the two extremes there are many variations with respect to permitting observation of adult sex, indulgence in child sex, and self-stimulation. All members of the Pukapukan household sleep in the same room under one mosquito net, and although some parents wait until they think the children are asleep, there are frequent opportunities for youngsters to observe sexual activities.[7] In most societies, however, couples seek some sort of seclusion for sexual intercourse.[8] This undoubtedly serves as assurance against interruptions.

As a result of such great differences in sexual training, adult members of different societies have quite varied opinions as to what is proper or normal or immoral or unnatural in sexual relations.[9] An adult may be quite shocked or perplexed at the attitudes and customs of another people. This is clearly shown in a letter by a mother in Rhodesia, in which she expresses feelings of disbelief at the Western taboo of co-family sleeping. "Our quarters here consist of one room, and naturally we all sleep in it." She further explains that their child is very much aware of adult sex, but that neither she nor her husband had ever thought that it would be harmful to him. "My husband and I were brought up in the same fashion. It hasn't given my husband a complex about sex." She ends her perplexed letter by asking the American doctor to whom this letter was directed, "And what is an Oedipus complex?"[10]

It is certainly not my intention to advocate parental sexual relations in the presence of one's children or any children. However, I have included this brief cross-cultural sample of the primal act to illustrate that just because our society feels it is immoral or damaging to the psyche—as children in the parental bed is thought to be—it may not in fact be so. These examples show that, in fact, other peoples do just that which our culture discourages and yet seem to produce quite stable individuals.

We have to accept the fact that, in our society, children's observation of their parents' sexual activities is not accepted; our style of living, morals, and taboos are not designed to compensate for this. But parents who enjoy sleeping with their children have found no difficulty in making other arrangements for sexual relations. A surprising number indicated that maturity, good humor, or patience plays an important part in their adaptability.

One mother emphasized the non-urgency of it all. If the child awakens or just plainly doesn't want to go to sleep, the sexual relations will have to be forgotten for that day. She comments, "There is always tomorrow, or next week. Don't blame postponement on the child." She further emphasized that, since they have two teenagers, she and her husband have found there to be many indications for foregoing immediate expression of sexual love. Sometimes one of the children wants to stay up and talk, or wanders around the house late at night. "It helps if you're not obsessed with the idea that sexual relations *must* take place. If you're going to be married for a lifetime, sooner or later you'll get around to whatever has to be postponed right now."

Some parents feel that using the living room or cozy den, with wine and soft music, adds pleasant variety. Others move to a spare bed in the house, or move the child or children who were in their bed in with other siblings. With the extraordinary depth of sleep that occurs in the first half of the night, sleeping children are often unaware of even being transported by their parents.[11]

Some families begin the night with the children away from the parental bed. This gives the parents a few hours of privacy. A mother of a large family wrote, "With seven children, intimate moments require planning and sometimes plotting." And one father answered, "If the interest is great enough, a way can be found."

Another young father replied, "I used to think it was my privilege as a husband to sleep with my wife in one bed, by ourselves. However, I now realize that when a man begets children, he is no longer merely a husband, he is also a father with the responsibilities of a father. And my wife is no longer only a wife, she is now a mother, with the responsibilities of a mother. We have responsibilities now in which personal wants will, at times, have to be foregone."

And a thoughtful mother commented on the effect of children on her sexual relationship with her husband: "Sometimes children inter- fere if you are referring to direct sexual intercourse. If sexual relation- ship refers to the total love relationship of sexually mature adults, then, no, since rearing our children is a primary aspect of our love and our relationship. Of course, expression of this love, though pref- erably physical, at times does have to suffice with verbal contact. It is the harmony of purpose rather than physical attraction which gives our marriage a solid foundation."

It is not only the presence of children, whether in the parental bed or not, which results in the foregoing of impulsive sexual relations. Many parents choose not to subject themselves to the known and unknown physical danger or moral responsibilities of artificial contraception. When they wish to limit the size of their family or postpone pregnancy, they use the highly effective method of natural family planning. This method is based on the bodily changes that take place within the woman, which indicate the fertile and infertile stages during the menstrual cycle. Natural family planning requires abstaining from sexual intercourse during certain days of a woman's menstrual cycle. When used correctly, this method can be, according to Kippley, more effective than the use of condoms or a diaphragm, and as effective as the Pill. It is considered to be more effective than the mini-Pill and the IUD, which are not as effective as the older and larger dosage pills. It has now been established that both the Pill and the IUD are abortifacts.

Those breastfeeding mothers who wish to benefit from the natural infertility through breastfeeding are strongly advised to take their babies to bed with them. The child will suck frequently during the night, and further secure the suppression of ovulation. This is part of the "total mothering" picture that Sheila Kippley has described in her book, *Breastfeeding and Natural Child Spacing: The Ecology of Natural Mothering.*

Many couples have found a new depth and meaning in their marriages when practicing natural family planning. Several years ago one such couple wished to share with others the meaning and knowledge they had obtained in their search for an effective natural method. Thus Sheila and John Kippley founded the Couple to Couple League (P.O. Box 11084, Cincinnati, Ohio 45211). Their manual, *The Art of Natural Family Planning,* has proven to be "the answer" for an increasing number of couples.

Abstaining from sexual intercourse, whether because of a nursing baby, a child in need, or to prevent pregnancy, has given many couples a chance to mature and grow in their love for each other and other members of the family.

Parents of a very young breastfeeding infant may have noticed a mysterious occurrence during sexual relations. In an article in *Psychology Today*, Dr. Krebs tells of an experience that he encountered with both of his breastfed children. As soon as he and his wife began to make love, the newborn would wake up, begin to whimper, and soon break into a full cry. The baby's awakening seemed to be unrelated to any other cause, such as hunger, noise, or movement. Three months after the birth of the first child, the mother conceived again. Baby was put on a bottle and stopped waking up when the parents were having sexual relations.[12] The bond between Mother and Baby was broken.

In response to this article, the following letter was submitted to *Psychology Today.*

Richard Krebs, M.D., has made some fascinating observations on infants awakening during parental sexual activity. I have been curious about this phenomenon from two points of view; first, as a mother of two breastfed children; and second, as an independent student of genetically-predetermined behavior patterns in human beings, particularly the mother-child relationships.

As a La Leche League counselor, in extensive contact with large numbers of nursing mothers, I agree that this phenomenon is quite common. Having read of Jane Gooddall's observations of chimpanzees, in which the young physically interfere with males' copulation attempts with the juveniles' mothers (to the extent of even knocking them off), I wondered if this was another of the inherited behavior patterns. Indeed, I would go so far as to speculate that perhaps *Homo sapiens'* apparent proclivity towards privacy and nighttime sexual encounters might have been a reaction towards this juvenile interference, responding to the simultaneous development of sexual behavior sustaining the continuous pair-bond (which the chimps do not have).

Incidentally, I would also go so far as to disagree with the hypothesis that it is the odor of the mother's milk which arouses the infant. The simple test of this would be to have the mothers express their milk, while near the sleeping infants. If others' experience is like my own, I would guess that the infants would not awaken. Yet the same infants would awaken if the mother engaged in sexual intercourse in a separate room. It is my temporary hypothesis that this awakening is based upon a psychic extrasensory phenomenon. I believe it is possible that the mother is in constant mental contact with the child, and that sexual behavior so distracts her that the connection is broken, and the infant awakens "seeking" its mother.

I would further guess that if the mother allowed the child to remain in the bed near her during her sexual activity the child would not awaken. This would support the theory that the awakening is related to being close to the mother, rather than to prevent conception. Indeed the fact that conception is greatly, if not almost totally, prevented by continuous lactation would indicate that that mechanism was already accounted for. What natural selection has not been able to account for is the apparently unique mammalian pattern in humans to leave their totally helpless infants in separate sleeping areas from the mothers. I am guessing that the awakening is the infant's way of insuring that the mother doesn't forget about it or abandon it.[13]

Certainly a thought-provoking letter. This peculiar mother-child relationship might be another manifestation of that mysterious link mentioned earlier, when a nursing mother wakes up in anticipation of her child's awakening. Or the strange occurrence related by nursing mothers — that of having a let-down at the same time their babies start crying, which is nothing unusual except that they may be doing their shopping while their babies are at home.

This leads one to further speculate about an inherent wisdom of nature — that it would be better for the mother not to have sexual relations until her child is older so as not to risk pregnancy while he is too young. It is probably for this reason that some cultures feel that the sexual relationship between husband and wife should be held off until the youngest of their children is two or three (in some cultures, even four or five). It is also important for the husband to realize that a new mother is not always all that interested in intercourse. This misunderstanding has lead to a great deal of tension between married couples. The husband feels rejected. The wife feels guilty and misunderstood. The Hollywood stereotype of the sexually-interested woman has been disrupted, and each wonders what is wrong with the other. There may not be anything wrong with her. She is simply going through one of the many physical and emotional stages that she, as a female, will go through during her lifetime. Monthly ovulation and menstruation, pregnancy and lactation, and finally, menopause, all bring with them changes in mood, energy output, and sexual drive.

Many believe that parents should have their own private bedroom for sexual relationships and quiet talk. This is deemed a necessity for a sound, happy marriage. In our society, most couples "enjoy" a considerable amount of bedroom privacy, since most children sleep away from the master bedroom. Yet, in 1960, the divorce rate was twenty-six divorces per every one hundred marriages. And a mere fifteen years later, in 1975, a new record had been set: forty-eight divorces per every one hundred marriages.[14] Fortunately, since the mid '70's the divorce rate has leveled out and has even declined somewhat. (U.S. News and World Report, Oct. 21, 1985, pg. 12.)

For parents who agree to co-family sleeping, there seems to be no particular problem in wanting to talk for a while before going to sleep. If the conversation revolves around a subject that the children should not hear, then it is discussed before going to bed. Otherwise, parents remarked, the children frequently sleep through their conversations.

If the youngsters should awaken, they simply listen, or join in the conversation. When a child sleeps with his parents, there need not be the fear of, "suppose he wakes up, we'll never get him back to sleep!" Many children all too eagerly snuggle up in the dark of the night, quickly falling asleep against another person.

When all is said and done, the proponents of separate sleeping arrangements produce one final argument: what about incest? My answer: should my husband or I deprive our children of love and security just because a few emotionally-maladjusted adults have sex with their children? Virginia Satir, author of *People Making* and a nationally-known family therapist, wrote, "If you want hanky-panky going on in your family, play down affection and have lots of taboos about sex. I can say that, without exception, any person I have seen with problems in sexual gratification in marriage, or who was homosexual, promiscuous, or who was arrested for any sexual crime, grew up with these kinds of taboos against sex. I'll go even further. Anyone whom I have seen with any kind of coping problems or emotional illness also grew up with taboos about sex."

Incest is not a universal taboo. We are dealing more with a person's inability to abide by the rules, regulations, and moral standards of the society in which he lives. The more emotionally-stable a person is, the easier it is for him to abide by a group's ethics, provided they are sound. And so we go right back to that basic human question: how do we rear emotionally-stable persons? This book supports one method aimed toward a holistic approach to child rearing.

12

Special Circumstances

Speak for the child because he can't always speak for himself.

"In the case of our adopted child," says one mother, "we felt that extra cuddling and togetherness during the hours in bed was the best way to break through emotional barriers. This child is bottlefed. I also lie down to bottlefeed him and cuddle at least once a day."

This approach also applies to the foster child, many of whom, like the adopted child, may have been very much deprived of the intimacy that is so necessary for optimum human development.

In her book, *Relactation: A Guide to Breastfeeding the Adopted Baby,* Elizabeth Hormann encourages adoptive mothers to take their babies to bed with them. This will not only result in the benefit of frequent nursing (thus additional stimulation to the breast, with an increase in milk production) but will also serve as a stimulation of the biological mother-child relationship. While frequent nursing does have a good effect on milk supply, it is this relationship that is the essence of nursing.[1]

In private correspondence, Mrs. Hormann referred to the many mothers who wrote that they keep their adopted babies with them all night to give them the body contact they may have missed in foster homes and institutions.

With the foregoing information in this book, it is clear that above all, the foster or adopted child should be welcomed, not only into his new home, but into the family or siblings' bed as well, so that he will truly feel like part of that family. "You have touched me. I have grown." How especially applicable to these children.

A mother wrote me:

> We were expecting our third child when we met Greg, a six-month-old, bi-racial baby. Greg was the younger brother of Jenny, our first adopted child. Jenny was then two years old.

Greg was a beautiful black baby, with large brown eyes and a sweet passive nature. Since he was related to our Jenny, we applied to adopt him, also. After eight months of concern for this little fellow, we were told we could not adopt him. He was placed in a Permanent Foster Care home. Although this was to have been a lifetime placement, it lasted only a year. Greg was then placed in another home and this placement, too, lasted only a year. By this time he was considered to be emotionally disturbed, and after a brief period of hospitalization he was placed in a diagnostic foster home for evaluation. He was by then three years old. By the grace of God, the mother who ran the diagnostic home realized that this was the child we had wanted to adopt, and she called us.

We could hardly contain our excitement at being able to see him again. Yet, we were filled with sorrow when we saw the sad physical and emotional condition into which he had deteriorated. He had changed so much. But when I picked him up, my arms remembered him and I knew that deep within him he was still that sweet baby. We immediately re-established contact with the welfare department and requested again to adopt him.

We were turned down many times. One reason, claimed the welfare department, was that we already had four children, and a child with this many emotional problems would need special attention. But we felt that having four children who would give him just that much more love and attention was an asset, not a liability.

Finally, after many months of prayerful perseverance, Greg was placed in our home for adoption.

What a joy we knew as we brought him into the loving circle of brothers and sisters who had awaited the arrival of their new brother for so long!

By this time, Greg was nearly four years old. Among his problems were the inability to keep food down, and to sleep through the night. It was also difficult for him to accept the normal, loving touching that goes on in a close family. He had always been expected to sleep by himself in his own room. In our family we have no such "luxury," and quite soon, as he slept with one of his siblings, the insomnia problems disappeared. We also gave him backrubs. But while his sleep and eating problems improved, he regressed in many other accomplishments.

His independence rapidly deteriorated. He could no longer dress himself. He began to speak in baby talk. But we followed through and tried to fulfill each need as it arose.

Greg is now a healthy, cheerful, active eight-year-old. He enjoys a lot of physical contact, and doesn't think that a room of his own would be a privilege. That is just as well because with seven children, doubling up is something that we take for granted.

It is a pleasure to see how easy it is now for Greg to give love, how natural it is for him to put his arm around his little three-year-old brother Joey, and gently guide him, or sit him on his lap and read him a story. It is also just as natural for him to wrestle and play football with his thirteen-year-old brother Jeff. It means so much to us to observe the true inner independence that has developed in our Greg.

A large family necessitates closeness and that has been a blessing to all of us because it has encouraged us to re-evaluate our priorities and to relate to each other in terms of meeting emotional needs. Many of these needs are met through the concerned touch of someone who cares.

My husband's and my own background is middle-class Swedish and English. This type of close relationship was not predominant in our cultural heritage. Experiencing this relationship, therefore, has been a lesson that we have been learning as we go along.

It has taken us fifteen years of child rearing to come to this point. Our first child, Tammy, came into our bed in the morning after she awakened. Our second child, Jeff, came into our bed during the night when he was old enough to crawl out of his crib. And so it went. Our three-year-old has slept with us every night since birth, although now he is spending an occasional night with an older brother or sister.

We wish now that we had been this casual and relaxed right from the beginning. We were silly enough at one time to think that we had to move from a two-bedroom home to a three-bedroom home when we had both a baby boy and a two-year-old girl. Afterwards we found to our chagrin that they did not like being in separate rooms and for a period of years we had a "spare" room, the room without which we thought we just could not do.

As we have grown and changed, we like to think that our changed values have had an impact on our older children, too. Perhaps we will not know to what extent this has taken place until they have children of their own. At the very least, it has given them an alternative approach to child rearing, rather than just accepting society's current values. This lesson alone is part of the most precious heritage we can give to our children.

This family closeness can undoubtedly have its positive effects on a step-parent as well.

Another situation occurring more and more frequently in this country is the single-parent family: usually a mother and child. Should a child who finds himself in that situation be allowed to sleep with his mother? Well, are we going to treat each child as if his parent is emotionally-maladjusted, or should we assume that most parents are quite capable of knowing right from wrong and concern ourselves with the welfare of the child? As stated earlier in this book, no matter what situation the child finds himself in, his need for love and security does not change. Therefore, the child *should* be allowed to sleep with his parent. An only child was once asked if she got a little lonesome sleeping by herself. She answered, "I get a lot of lonesome." It is also up to the parent (and not the school system) to teach his or her child the moral obligations of our society. This is best done at home, and at an early age.

Parents with a water bed may be concerned about the young child sliding between the mattress and the sideboard. One family solved this problem by stuffing a blanket into the space.

Many of the questions asked and concerns voiced are presented by those who have not experienced a family bed situation. But one bewildering question comes only from those who have a family bed. Why do babies insist on crawling up onto the pillows and sleeping sideways? It is indeed a mystery. But the answer most likely lies in the fact that we dress them too warmly.

What if the young child, who is accustomed to sleeping with someone, has to go to the hospital? There is no question that every effort should be made for a member of the family to stay with that child at all times. This also means sleeping by him in the same hospital room, or even in his bed. Parents must never be made to feel less needed when their child is hospitalized, for they alone can serve as a sign of normalcy in a very abnormal situation.

The possibility of hospitalization should never be the reason for not allowing the child into the parental bed, or into his siblings' beds. This is too rare an occasion.

It is known that, when under the stress of childbirth, many parturient women react only to the voice of their assisting husbands, especially when giving birth in that strange environment surrounded by strangers: the hospital situation. Isn't it possible that children, also, when under the stress of illness and the strange surroundings of a hospital, will respond better to medical orders when these have been repeated by a parent?

The biological connection between a parent and his child, says Salk, enhances communication and makes the parent especially well-geared to the job of caring for his own child.[2]

Aside from the great benefits to the child, it is of psychological benefit to the parent himself to be with and care for his child during the latter's illness. Wanting to "do something," if only to stroke his hand, is a very natural desire of a parent when he is concerned about his child. Separation would only lead to frustration and perhaps, on the part of the child, a feeling of worthlessness. In this light, hospital administrators need to re-evaluate very thoroughly the common practice of separating the sick individual from his family and restricting the much-needed loving atmosphere, which only a family member can truly give, to a few visiting hours. A hospital stay may be short. A resulting emotional trauma may, however, be long lasting.

A young child may not be able to express the dire need he has to be touched and cared for by a loving member of the family. But an adult can and we should learn from his experiences.

The mother of a friend of mine had to undergo a very serious operation. After the surgery she was in intensive care for several days. The patient was in extremely critical condition, but her daughter convinced the physician to allow her to be with her mother. During those critical days my friend stayed with her mother for the greater part of the day, and although the patient was not responding to anything that was said to her, my friend continually touched her mother by lightly stroking her hand, arm, or head. The mother recuperated, and after she was well again, told her daughter that during those first few days after surgery, she was in such extreme pain that frequently she wanted to die. The only thing that gave her courage and hope was the loving, gentle touch of her daughter's hand.

The physician was so impressed by this that he now encourages the immediate families of his patients to be with them when they are in the hospital.

The wonderful book, *Young Children in Hospital* by Dr. James Robertson, gives a thoroughly-documented description of the deep need of the pre-schooler for the presence of his mother, especially during a time of hospitalization. It repeatedly points out that the child who has the constant presence of one of his parents is a happy patient, and when he returns home he picks up where he left off, with little sign that he has been away.

No matter how kind the nurses and doctors are, a child needs the familiar security of his mother, in whom he places all his trust. Should she leave him, he becomes grief-stricken, unable to understand why those whom he needs so very much have let him down. He experiences a sense of loss and abandonment. There has been a serious failure within that environment of love and security, which the family provided before he went into the strange hospital environment. He may seem to have adjusted to his hospital situation, but to a careful observer he will appear frightened, lonesome, and in urgent need of his mother.

Parents whose child needs to be hospitalized are strongly urged to read this book before their child's admission, or contact Children in Hospital, 31 Wilshire Park, Needham, MA 02192.

Hospitalization of the mother can be extremely upsetting as far as the emotional welfare of the child, or children, is concerned. However, enlightened hospital administrators and personnel are beginning to recognize the importance of continued family interrelationships. Children are permitted to visit their mothers, and fathers have unrestricted visiting privileges.

I personally know three mothers who were permitted to have their breastfeeding babies (one was three weeks old, one seven months old, and one twelve months old) as soon after surgery as they were capable of nursing. With the full cooperation of the nursing staff and doctors, each was permitted to have her baby in bed with her, also during the night. All three mothers were accustomed to sleeping with their children. The hospital personnel made special comments on how well the babies "behaved," and how quickly the mothers seemed to recuperate. In each case, several of the mother's friends helped out in the hospital room by taking care of the baby—i.e., changing him, playing with him, or taking him home for a few hours. "After all," remarked one understanding nurse, "nature does go on."

13

Nighttime Is for Sleeping!

Life is a perpetual instruction in cause and effect.

Emerson

It is quiet. It is dark. It is night. Somewhere a young child awakens and speaks: "Mama?" Mama stirs in her sleep. She reaches over and takes the child's hand. "Mama, I have to go to the bathroom."

"Fine, Sweetheart. Just slip quietly off the foot of the bed, and go to the bathroom. Mama will stay awake for you."

The youngster stands up. "But I want to go that way," pointing sideways to where other members of the family are sleeping.

"You will wake everyone up. Now please go quietly off the end of the bed."

"No! I want to go that way!"

Papa's dreams *are* interrupted. All are no longer asleep. All is not well.

Should a situation like this be tolerated? Of course not. Our role as parents does not stop at night and resume in the morning. A situation like this should be no more tolerated than if the child were in his own room and started disturbing the quiet night, or yelling in church, throwing food at the dinner table, or refusing to comply with family rules.

A mother from Minnesota once said, "Think of how much animosity is directed at children who are ill-behaved. I don't want my children to have to bear this type of burden, so I teach them how to behave in our world."

Just because children are welcomed into the family bed does not mean that they should be permitted to come and go as they please, when they please, and how they please. Their manner shouldn't be disruptive of the smooth and peaceful functioning of the family. Of course we must always remember the emotional age of the child, his needs, and his capabilities. The child who awakens the family with his crying because he is in pain, or uncomfortable from a cold, should not be treated the same way as the child who decides to run in and out of his parents' bedroom or use the bed as a trampoline, or willfully awakens the others with loud talking, balking, or giggling.

The family that is not used to sleeping together may not be aware of the nighttime activities of young children. According to Luce and Segal, it is not unusual for a child of two or three years to stand up in bed, sit, or talk. This usually happens during a very deep sleep, and the child may be extremely hard to awaken. The child is not purposely disturbing the family. And this behavior is not abnormal. It is important for parents to realize this so that they will not reprimand a child who may be in a deep sleep, and totally unaware of his doings.[1]

A six-month-old baby who is still awake for some midnight philosophizing should certainly not be treated the same way as the four-year-old who is gauging his parents. Nor should the ten-year-old be treated like a four-year-old. He may have some real emotional problems (real to *him*) that are keeping him awake, and about which he needs to talk right then and there. (But at one a.m., you ask? Yes, Mother!) As a matter of fact, one parent told me that these midnight talks were most revealing and most helpful with her teenage youngster.

How, then, should one deal with a situation of this type? The child should be made to understand that the family sleeps at night. We all need our sleep, and it is not fair for one or more persons to willfully or thoughtlessly keep others awake. Daytime is for playing, laughing, talking, eating. Nighttime is for sleeping.

There are a great many books on the subject of child rearing and methods of discipline. Many of these books claim to have the ultimate answer to rearing children. Through my reading I have concluded, however, that it is not necessarily the method used, but the security, consistency, love, and respect exhibited to children and others that will have long lasting, good results in rearing them.

We all strive toward a common goal; peace and harmony and health. There are many roads leading toward this goal, and one may be no more right than the other. Whether one person or many people follow that road, it is valid as long as it leads to the goal without violence. Above all, each must not blindly succumb to another person's way, but have faith in and use his own head and heart.

In our efforts to rear our children and do what is right for them, we make mistakes. Child rearing involves one decision-making episode after another, and being able to live with their outcomes. With no centuries-old methods to guide us, it is no wonder that we make errors. Until a hundred years ago or so, child rearing customs were handed down from a mother to her children. A new mother could usually turn to her own mother for advice. Then, for better or for worse, child rearing customs began to change.

It is not surprising that parents are hesitant and wavering in their guiding actions and that they should experience a feeling of frustration or guilt if they do not live up to the ideal goal any of the child rearing methods set forth. The parent does not feel, "Look at what I am doing to my *child*," but rather, "Look what *I* am doing to my child." And this, of course, is a tremendous responsibility and awareness of one's doings and capabilities.

Much of the misbehavior of today's children is due to boredom, lack of playmates, and a desire to fulfill a direct human relationship—love—which is not, for one reason or another, forthcoming. It might be helpful to ask, "Why is the child acting this way?" Keep communication open and you may be surprised at the answers. Listen!

One proud mother told me of the following occurrence in her family. After a particularly trying time, her husband sat down with their twelve-year-old son and asked him why he had been exhibiting such ill behavior. After careful questioning, the boy's troubles were revealed. And afterwards, it was the son who said to his father, "Dad, we are like a Walkie-Talkie. As long as we don't get too far away from one another and keep communications going, we'll be doing all right."

As we grow with our children, we begin to mellow, mature, and see our children and our relationships with them in a more realistic nature. When our first-born was two years old, she was *already* two. When our second-born was that age, we said that she was *only* two. We realized the physical, emotional, and mental capabilities of the second child more realistically.

Above all, take a risk and trust your child. It's a marvelous feeling.

14

Conclusion

The strongest principle of growth lies in human choice.

George Eliot

At the end of every winter, when tender new leaves appear on the trees and shrubs, when the robins return, and the daffodils bloom once more, we are surprised again that indeed time did not stand still after all. Winter has come to pass.

Winter is a time of intimacy, of cuddling, of feeling cozy near a warm fire. But, as beautiful as winter is, it does at times seem long.

So, too, an infant will grow and slip out of your arms, will grow some more and slip out of your bed, will grow again and slip out of your home. Each phase will pass—just as winter passes into spring, summer into autumn.

"We have grown together as parents to an understanding that our children need us at night," wrote a parent. "There have been times when the learning-growing process was difficult, sometimes for me, sometimes for my husband. It is often very beautiful, sometimes trying, but always worthwhile. The parental bed has become a *family bed*, which does not take away from the bed of love, but adds to it."

Should we be concerned about our neighbors' opinions if we have found a solution for our family situation? The importance lies in finding arrangements which, with a mature understanding of each other's and the children's needs, will make everyone happy. The acceptance of this situation will lead to a relaxed, happy atmosphere. "Happiness is the atmosphere in which all good affections grow" (Thomas Bray).

Ashley Montagu quoted James Plant as saying, "a conformity that is based on love will be free to develop into nonconformities, for the mentally-healthy individual will not be bound to standards that conflict with his view of what is right."[1]

There is room in our society for experimentation, which can enrich and strengthen family life. There is no reason to assume that our culture has seized upon "an eternal sanity" that will stand the test of time as a solitary solution to the human problem.[2] Families are disregarding social customs, and those who sleep together have found it has enriched and strengthened their family life.

With the increasing popularity of the small family, it is especially important for the young child to spend some time in his parents' bed at night and later sleep with his sibling or siblings— if not in the same bed, then at least in the same room. With our small families and large houses, it is so easy to become literally "out-of-touch" with one another.

Most of us can identify with the feeling of comfortable togetherness that somehow permeates the air when other loving people are present in the room. It is a pretty lonesome feeling to be by oneself, in a quiet room, surrounded by the darkness of night.

Giving of ourselves should not be determined by a clock or schedule, but by human needs. In our society we tend to separate ourselves from our children instead of allowing our children to separate themselves from *us* when they are ready. We should be the tree, strong and well-rooted, and they the seedlings which, when ready, will fall away with all the potentialities of a new tree.

There is much evidence to indicate the great importance of a long, fulfilled transition phase for the development of an emotionally-stable person, one who will be *inwardly* strong. A baby's sleeping with its mother for the first few years of life is an important aspect of the smooth functioning of the transition phase. Children who then initiate the separation will do so contentedly, whereas the child who is forced to leave before he is ready may suffer from anxiety and the fear of losing his mother.[3]

Throughout a person's life, he must have consideration, respect, and the ability to live in harmony with the world. The preparation for this maturity begins the moment a child is born. Sleeping together is an active part of this educational process.

The need for privacy cannot be overlooked and parents have every right to it. However, this should not be placed above the needs of the children, nor satisfied in spite of the children, for they are our primary responsibility.

Although life seems easier for the modern family than for that of our great-grandparents, a lot of strain is placed on parents today. When the extended family lived together, a youngster in need of attention could always turn to another relative if his mother were not available. Children today have the same need for human attention; however, no matter how many children are in the family, there is usually only Mom and Dad around. Neither parent should have to be all-bearing, and yet there is no other choice. I believe we should seriously reconsider the great beneficial and wonderful position grandparents can fill. We need them as much as they need us.

Our children are constantly reminded that they should share. Even if they don't want to, we make them share, for not sharing is socially unacceptable. Adults share too, says Montagu, until to do so becomes a burden or interferes with what they desire; then they rebel.[4]

Personal property need not be shared, but a child has every right to his share of the love and security of his parents when he needs it, be it during the day in the kitchen, or at night in bed. And these precious years of sharing oneself with children are so short. With fewer pregnancies and longer life spans, most couples can now anticipate almost twenty years of "child-free" living.

At least 4,000 years ago an Egyptian scribe wrote of the disrespect, lack of control, and generally appalling behavior of the young people of that day. The gulf between the generations of today, however, has been matched few times in recorded history.[5] Perhaps a return to co-family sleeping would help to narrow this gap.

There is no such thing as rearing children in a "perfect" way. However, there are certain elements of child rearing that seem to lead more successfully to the growth of a happy, healthy person. Natural childbirth, breastfeeding, co-family sleeping, good nutrition, love, and respect are some of these elements. Certainly children have been reared without some, or perhaps most of these. There are many fine children who did not sleep with their parents, who were bottlefed, whose mothers worked, but who received lots of love and respect from their parents. They were listened to.

It would be thoughtless to simply say, "Give your children that which they need," for deep within many of us lie needs that were not fulfilled during our own infancy, needs which, even as adults, we are still trying to fulfill—needs that are so strong that they surface when we are faced with our own children's demands. It would be thoughtless because true maturing comes from within ourselves, not from without. We frequently read, "If you don't want to take full responsibility for your children, then you are not ready and should not have children."

But it is strangely wonderful that, for many of us, our very own children are the ones who make us more mature. They allow us to experience more fully that which our own parents may have left incomplete. They awaken within us dormant instincts, dormant selves, even though it may take several children before this happens.

I used to feel greatly resentful toward those who told me, "You'll change when you have children. Your life will change." I felt resentful because I felt threatened. Perhaps I felt threatened that another person was going to control me, change me. I liked the way things were. But children can be the greatest blessing that one ever has. When one has had children, one has had a chance to grow in ways not otherwise possible. Let it not be said, therefore, "You *must* grow. You *must* mature. You must not have children until you are ready." For then we may wait forever. Rather, let it suffice to say, "*Allow* yourself to grow, to mature *with* your children."

It is through our children that I gained a deeper understanding of my own nature, and of the beauty life can give. If children can give this to their parents, should we not fully reap the fruit of their being?

Let's, therefore, re-unite the family and say, "our house," "our dining room," "our bedroom." And let us say, "I have respect for you—not only for your things, but for you as a person. I'll be quiet if you want to sleep. I'll rub your back. I'll not sprawl my things all over if there is not enough room." This respect has a chance to grow when we live together, not when we are separated behind doors. We learn to live together by doing just that, living together, not by separating. Sleep is so wonderful, let's share it with our loved ones, our children. It was meant to be that way.

Epilogue

Children have slept with their parents since the dawn of mankind, and it is only in the last century that this custom has been called into question as harmful. In this remarkable little book, the first of its kind, Mrs. Thevenin has illustrated how the breakdown in this wholesome, natural custom has come about, and why its restoration is so important to the emotional health and stability of future generations.

The breakdown in family sleeping parallels the alienation, depersonalization and dehumanization that have followed the development of industrialization. Young people have been separated from ancestral homes to flock to the city for jobs, where too often they can be "cogs in a machine," and do not even know their next door neighbors.

Women were alienated from their own body processes, anesthetized in labor, separated from their infants at birth. Anesthetics and the accompanying problems necessitated more hospital births, separating the woman and baby from the father. The alienated infant was kept in a room separate from his mother and fed with a bottle. On his return home, the alienation was continued by being put in his "own" bed, often in a separate room.

The trends toward dehumanization continue with the artificial premature severing of mother and infant through widespread abortion, the possibilities of artificial insemination, and the current research toward the development of conception in a test tube and artificial pregnancies in laboratory conditions. It is all too easy for needed research and helpful techniques to become the "norm!" Already there are legal attempts in some nations to control the number of children in a family and mandatory pre-school, where children are reared by the state almost from birth.

How greatly we need to return to an outlook which builds relationships, rather than moves toward destroying them! The infant who has slept with his mother for nine months prenatally needs time to be weaned from her presence more gradually, and needs time in which to build a relationship with his father who has been away at work all day, and needs opportunity to gain confidence in his own fatherhood through the closeness of a sleeping infant.

How much a child is in the parental bed will differ from family to family, and even from child to child. Those of us who have let our children sleep with us have seen them grow into warm, secure, loving adults. Our six children were in and out of the parental bed. But we can really be grateful to Mrs. Thevenin for encouraging mothers and fathers to follow their hearts, rather than the "experts," and know that it is right!

Helen Wessel
Author of *Childbirth and the Family* (Harper and Row, 1973); Editor (with Harlan Ellis, M.D.) of *Childbirth Without Fear* by the late Grantly Dick-Read (4th ed. Harper and Row, 1972); President of Bookmates International, Inc.

About the Author

Tine Thevenin was born in the Netherlands and educated there and in the United States. She is the mother of two children and was, for a number of years, a counselor for La Leche League, an organization committed to a belief in the importance of good mothering through breastfeeding.

Mrs. Thevenin strongly feels that the strength of this book lies in the fact that it was written by a mother; and mothering, she believes, is a special profession that can only be learned at home, with children.

Footnotes

1. A Rediscovery

1—*Psychology Today.* Newton, N. "Breastfeeding," Jn. 1968.

3. Some Parents Hesitate

1—Salk, Lee. *What Every Child Would Like His Parents To Know.* N.Y. McKay Comp. Inc. 1972, p. 106.

2—"Infant Care." Children's Bureau Publ. No. 8, 1967, U.S. Dept. of Health, Educ., and Welfare, Wash. D.C., p. 25.

3—Brazelton, T. Berry. *Infants and Mothers.* N.Y. Dell Publ. 1969, p. 9.

4—Ibid.

5—Janov, Arthur. *The Primal Scream.* N.Y. Dell Publ. 1970.

6—"What's A Mother To Do?" *Newsweek.* Sept. 23, 1968, p. 68.

7—Spock, Benjamin. *Baby and Child Care.* N.Y. Pocket Books. 1968, p. 169.

8—Ibid, p. 196.

9—Ibid, p. 355.

10—Luce, Gay, and Segal, Julius. *Insomnia.* Garden City, N.Y. Doubleday and Comp. 1969, p. 197.

11—Ibid, p. XI.

12—Gersh, Marvin J. *How To Raise Children At Home In Your Spare Time.* Greenwich, Conn. Fawcett Publ., Inc. 1966, p. 74.

13—"Ear Infection." *CEAN Today.* Aug. 1973. P.O. Box 20091, Minneapolis, Minn. 55420, p. 73.

14—"Facts About Sudden Infant Death Syndrome." National Foundation for Sudden Infant Death, 1501 Broadway, N.Y. 10036. 1970, p. 9.

15—Gerard, Alice. *Please Breastfeed Your Baby.* New American Library. Pocket Books. 1970, p. 97.

16—"Facts About Sudden Infant Death Syndrome." NFSID, 1501 Broadway, N.Y. 10036. 1970, p. 4.

17—Duluth, Minn. Newspaper. (Name of newspaper and date unknown.)

18—"Facts About Sudden Infant Death Syndrome." NFSID, 1501 Broadway, N.Y. 10036. 1970, p. 4.

19—"Crib Deaths." *LLL News.* Franklin Park, Ill., 1971, p. 89.

20—Aldrich, C. Anderson. *Babies are Human Beings,* p. 85.

21—"Facts About Sudden Infant Death Syndrome." NFSID, 1501 Broadway, N.Y. 1970, p. 5.

22—La Leche League International. *The Womanly Art of Breastfeeding.* 9616 Minneapolis Ave., Franklin Park, Ill. 60131. 1958, p. 83.

4.   The Importance of Sleeping Together

1—Montagu, Ashley. *Touching.* N.Y. Columbia Univ. Press. 1971, p. 79.

2—Montagu, Ashley. *Man: His First Million Years.* Mentor Book, N.Y. 1957, p. 88.

3—Montagu, Ashley. *On Being Human.* N.Y. Hawthorn Books. 1966, p. 93.

4—Montagu, Ashley. *Man: His First Million Years.* Mentor Book, N.Y. 1957, p. 88.

5—Salk, Lee and Kramer, Rita. *How to Raise a Human Being.* N.Y. Random House. 1969, p. 14.

6—Ratner, H. "Public Health Aspects of Breastfeeding." Section on pediatrics. Jn. 25, 1958. American Medical Association Annual Meeting. San Francisco, Ca. Distributed by LLLI, Franklin Park, Ill. 60131, p. 3.

7—Salk, Lee. *What Every Child Would Like His Parents To Know.* N.Y. McKay Comp. 1972, p. 1.

8—Janov, Arthur. *The Primal Scream.* N.Y. Dell Publ. 1970, p. 27.

9—Montagu, Ashley. *On Being Human.* N.Y. Hawthorn Books, 1966, p. 96.

10—Ibid.

11—"Waiting Game vs. Gaining Weight." LLLI reprint. LLLI, Franklin Park, Ill, p. 1.

12—Montagu, Ashley. "Some Factors in Family Cohesion." *Psychiatry,* Vol. 7. 1944, p. 350.

13—Ibid.

14—Montagu, Ashley. *Touching.* Columbia Univ. Press. N.Y. 1971, p. 22.

15—*National Geographic.* Aug. 1972, p. 244.

16—Montagu, Ashley. *Touching.* Columbia Univ. Press. N.Y. 1971, p. 247.

17—Ibid, p. 4.

18—Ratcliff, J.D. "I'm Joe's Skin." *Readers' Digest.*. 1972, p. 114.

19—Montagu, Ashley. *Touching.* Columbia Univ. Press. N.Y. 1971, p. 80.

20—Kenny, James and Schreiter, Robert. "Of Babies, Beds and Teddy Bears." *Marriage Magazine.* Jan. 1971, pp. 18–24.

21—Richardson, S.A. et al. *Childbearing: Its Social and Psychological Aspects.* Williams and Wilkens. 1967, p. 177.

22—Ibid, p. 186.

23—Ibid, p. 179.

24—Kenny, J. and Schreiter, R. "Of Babies, Beds and Teddy Bears." *Marriage Magazine.* Jan. 1971, p. 21.

25—*Psychology Today,* Newton, N. "Breastfeeding." Jn. 1968.

26—Montagu, Ashley. *Touching.* Columbia Univ. Press. N.Y. 1971, p. 287.

27—Luce, Gay and Segal, Julius. *Insomnia.* Garden City, N.Y. Doubleday and Comp. 1969, p. 163.

28—Bowlby, John. *Attachment and Loss,* Vol. 2: *Separation.* Basic Books. 1973, pp. 166–168.

29—Ibid, p. 167.

30—Luce, Gay and Segal, Julius. *Sleep.* Coward-McGann Inc. N.Y. 1966, p. 25.

31—Luce, Gay and Segal, Julius. *Insomnia.* Garden City, N.Y. Doubleday and Comp. 1969, p. 20.

32—Froehlich, Edwina. La Leche League of Minnesota, Third State Seminar Transcript. April, 1972. LLLI, Franklin Park, Ill. 60131.

33—Chisholm, Brock. *Prescription For Survival.* Columbia Univ. Press. N.Y. 1957, p. 40.

34—Salk, Lee. *What Every Child Would Like His Parents To Know.* N.Y. McKay Comp. 1972, p. 14.

35—Montagu, Ashley. *Touching.* Columbia Univ. Press. N.Y. 1971, p. 173.

36—Ribble, Margaret. *The Rights Of Infants.* Columbia Univ. Press. N.Y. 1965, p. 53.

37—Arnstein, Helene. "How Babies Learn To Wait." *Parents' Mag.* Dec. 1970.

38—Morris, Desmond. *Intimate Behavior.* Random House. N.Y. 1971, p. 103.

5. Need vs. Habit

1—Salk, Lee. "Role of the Heartbeat in the Relationship Between Mother and Infant." *Scientific American.* May, 1973, p. 29.

2—Montagu, Ashley. *Touching.* Columbia Univ. Press. N.Y. 1971, p. 289.

3—Janov, Arthur. *The Primal Scream.* Dell Publ. N.Y. 1970, p. 22.

4—"What Is A Mother To Do?" *Newsweek.* Sept. 23, 1968, p. 69.

5—Hymes, James. *Child Under Six.* Englewood Cliffs, N.J. Prentice Hall. 1963, p. 87.

6—Salk, Lee. *What Every Child Would Like His Parents To Know.* N.Y. McKay Comp. 1972, p. 42.

7—"Frequent Night Nursing of Toddlers and Clinging Dependence During the Day." LLL reprint No. 77. LLLI, Franklin Park, Ill. 60131, p. 3.

6.   Brief History of Childhood and Family Sleeping

1—Luce, Gay and Segal, Julius. *Sleep.* N.Y. Coward-McGann. 1966, p. 24.

2—Aries, P. *Centuries of Childhood.* N.Y. Knopf. 1962, p. 33.

3—Ibid, p. 34.

4—Ryerson, Alice. "Medical Advice on Child Rearing 1550–1900." *Harvard Ed. Review.* Vol. 31. No. 3, p. 313.

5—Aries, P. *Centuries of Childhood.* N.Y. Knopf. 1962, p. 34.

6—Ibid, p. 106.

7—Ibid, p. 394.

8—Luce, Gay and Segal, Julius. *Insomnia.* Garden City, N.Y. Doubleday and Comp. 1969, p. 152.

9—Kenny and Schreiter, "Of Babies, Beds and Teddy Bears." *Marriage Magazine.* Jan. 1971, p. 22.

10—Aries, P. *Centuries of Childhood.* N.Y. Knopf. 1962, p. 103.

11—Ibid, p. 106.

12—Ryerson, Alice. "Medical Advice on Child Rearing 1550–1900." *Harvard Ed. Review.* Vol. 31, No. 3, p. 302.

13—Aries. P. *Centuries of Childhood.* N.Y. Knopf. 1962, p. 115.

14—Ibid, p. 412.

15—Ibid, p. 400.

16—DeWees, W. *Treatise on the Physical and Medical Treatment of Children.* Philadelphia, Carey, Lea and Carey. 1829.

17—Stiles, H. *Bundling.* Albany Knickerbocker Publ. 1871, p. 106.

18—Ibid, p. 2.

19—Ibid, p. 65.

20—Kenny and Schreiter. "Of Babies, Beds and Teddy Bears." *Marriage Magazine.* Jan. 1971, p. 22.

21—Langer, L. and Langer, A. "The Pursuit of Happiness." (An American Comedy) N.Y. Samuel French. 1934, p. xxvii.

22—Stiles, H. *Bundling.* Albany Knickerbocker Publ. 1871, p. 65.

23—Ryerson, Alice. "Medical Advice on Child Rearing 1550–1900." *Harvard Ed. Review.* Vol. 31, No. 3, p. 302.

24—Stiles, H. *Bundling.* Albany Knickerbocker Publ. 1871, p. 79.

25—Ryerson, Alice. "Medical Advice on Child Rearing 1550–1900." *Harvard Ed. Review.* Vol. 31, No. 3, p. 302.

26—Ibid.

27—Luce, Gay and Segal, Julius. *Insomnia.* Garden City, N.Y. Doubleday and Comp. 1969, p. 153.

28—"What Is A Mother To Do?" *Newsweek.* Sept. 23, 1968, p. 68.

29—LLL of Minnesota, 3rd State Seminar, April 1972. Wessel, Helen. Available through LLLI, Franklin Park, Ill. 60131.

30—"What Is A Mother To Do?" *Newsweek.* Sept. 23, 1968, p. 68.

31—Nichols, J. *Safe Counsel.* Chicago, Ill. Franklin Publ. 1928, p. 132.
—Holt, L. Emmett, Jr. *Care and Feeding of Children.* N.Y. Appleton-Century Comp. 1943, p. 20.

32—Kenny and Schreiter. "Of Babies, Beds and Teddy Bears." *Marriage Magazine.* Jan. 1971, p. 23

33—Luce, Gay and Segal, J. *Insomnia.* Garden City, N.Y. Doubleday and Comp. 1969, p. 155.

34—Newton, N. *Family Book of Child Care.* N.Y. Harper and Row. 1957, p. 156.
—*Child and Family Quarterly* (see general index of magazine) Ed. Herbert Ratner, M.D., Box 508, Oak Park, Ill. 60303.

7.   Some Anthropological Observations

1—Erickson, Erik. *Childhood and Society.* N.Y. Norton and Comp. 1963, p. 112.

2—Hass, Hans. *The Human Animal.* N.Y. Putnam's Sons. 1970.

3—Elkin, A.P. *The Australian Aborigines: How To Understand Them.* London. 1945.
—Thomas, Elizabeth M. *The Harmless People.* N.Y. Knopf. 1959.

4—Kenny and Schreiter. "Of Babies, Beds and Teddy Bears." *Marriage Magazine.* Jan. 1971, p. 18.

5—Barry, H. III and Paxson, L.M. "Infancy and Early Childhood: Cross-Cultural Codes 2" *Ethnology.* Vol. 10, Oct. 1971.

6—Moloney, James. *Fear: Contagion and Conquest,* pp. 72–84.

7—Montagu, Ashley. *Touching.* Columbia Univ. Press. N.Y. 1971, p. 117.

8—Ibid, p. 249.
—Luce, Gay and Segal, Julius. *Sleep.* Coward-McGann. N.Y. 1966, p. 25.
—Johnston, Madeline. "Discipline or Indulgence?" *Parents' Mag.* July 1969.

9—Breetveld, J. "Mother and Child in Africa." *Psychology Today.* Feb. 1972, p. 63.

10—Montagu, Ashley. *Touching.* Columbia Univ. Press. N.Y. 1971, pp. 225, 233.

11—Montagu, Ashley. *On Being Human.* N.Y. Hawthorn Books. 1966, p. 86.

12—Mead, Margaret. *From The South Seas.* N.Y. Morrow. 1939.

8.   The Infant

1—Montagu, Ashley. "Some Factors in Family Cohesion." *Psychiatry.* Vol. 7, 1944, p. 351.

2—Montagu, Ashley. *Touching.* Columbia Univ. Press. N.Y. 1971, p. 65.

3—Ibid.

4—Newton, Niles. *Maternal Emotions.* N.Y. Medical Book Dept. of Harper and Row. 1955, p. 7.

5—Salk, Lee and Kramer, R. *How to Raise a Human Being.* N.Y. Random House. 1969, p. 7.

6—Ibid, p. 54.
   —Salk, Lee. *What Every Child Would Like His Parents To Know.* McKay Comp. N.Y. 1972, p. 6.

7—Albrecht, R. LLL of Minnesota Third State Seminar Transcript. April 1972. Available through LLLI, Franklin Park, Ill. 60131.

8—Brecher, R. "Why Some Mothers Reject Their Babies." *Redbook.* May, 1966, p. 49.

9—"On Nursing the Newborn . . . How Soon?" LLL reprint. LLLI, Franklin Park, Ill. 60131. 1972.

10—Pryor, Karen. *Nursing Your Baby.* N.Y. Pocket Books. 1973, p. 75.

11—Haire, Doris. *The Cultural Warping of Childbirth.* ICEA. Doris B. Haire, 251 Nottingham Way. Hillside, N.J. 1972, p. 27.
   —Albrecht, R. "Prepared Childbirth in Hospital." LLL of Minnesota Third State Seminar Transcript. April 1972.

12—Ribble, M. *The Rights of Infants.* Columbia Univ. Press N.Y. 1965, p. 18.

13—Montagu, A. *Touching.* Columbia Univ. Press. N.Y. 1971, p. 90.
   —Marlow, D. *Textbook of Pediatric Nursing.* Phil. Saunders Comp. 1969, p. 102.
   —Ziegel, Erna and V. Blarcom C. *Obstetric Nursing.* N.Y. McMillan Comp. 1972, p. 575.

14—Haire, D. *The Cultural Warping of Childbirth.* ICEA. Doris B. Haire, 251 Nottingham Way, Hillside, N.J. 1972.

15—Ibid, p. 7.

16—"On Nursing The Newborn . . . How Soon?" LLL reprint. LLLI, Franklin Park, Ill. 60131. 1972, p. 3.

17—Montagu, Ashley. *Touching.* Columbia Univ. Press. N.Y. 1971, p. 114.

18—Pryor, K. *Nursing Your Baby.* N.Y. Pocket Books. 1973, p. 46.

19—*LLL News.* Franklin Park, Ill. 60131. 1970, p. 70.

20—Janov, A. *The Feeling Child.* N.Y. Simon and Schuster. 1973, p. 27.

21—Kenny and Schreiter. "Of Babies, Beds and Teddy Bears." *Marriage Magazine.* Jan. 1971, p. 18.

22—Salk, Lee. "Role of the Heartbeat in the Relationship Between Mother and Infant." *Scientific American.* May, 1973, p. 29.

23—Salk, Lee and Kramer, R. *How to Raise a Human Being.* N.Y. Random House. 1969, p. 65.

24—Richardson, S. A. et al. *Childbearing: Its Social and Psychological Aspects.* Williams and Wilkens. 1967, p. 183.

25—Bowlby, J. *Attachment and Loss,* Vol. 2. *Separation.* Basic Books. 1973.

26—Salk, Lee and Kramer, R. *How to Raise a Human Being.* N.Y. Random House. 1969, p. 65.

27—Morris, D. *Intimate Behavior.* N.Y. Random House. 1971, p. 19.

28—Perkins, J. "Possible Causes of Crying and Frequent Nighttime Nursings." Minneapolis, Minn. 1972.

29—Morris, D. *Intimate Behavior.* N.Y. Random House, 1971, p. 25.

30—*LLL News.* Illinois Insert. March, 1973.

31—Luce, Gay and Segal, Julius. *Insomnia.* Garden City, N.Y. Doubleday Corp. 1969.

32—Ibid, p. 245.

33—Ibid.

34—*The Womanly Art of Breastfeeding.* LLL Manual. LLLI, Franklin Park, Ill. 60131. 1958, p. 61.

35—*LLL News.* Minnesota Insert. Vol. 15, No. 2. 1973.

36—Lorenz. *King Solomon's Ring.* N.Y. Coward-McGann, Inc. 1952.

9.   The Child Past Infancy

1—Montagu, Ashley. *Touching.* Columbia Univ. Press. N.Y. 1971, p. 253.

2—Kenny and Schreiter. "Of Babies, Beds and Teddy Bears." *Marriage Magazine.* Jan. 1971, p. 23.

3—Montagu, Ashley. *Touching.* Columbia Univ. Press. N.Y. 1971, p. 253.

4—Newton, Niles. *Family Book of Childcare,* N.Y. Harper and Row, 1951, p. 185.

5—Ibid, p. 188.

6—Ibid, p. 189.

7—Kenny and Schreiter. "Of Babies, Beds and Teddy Bears." *Marriage Magazine.* Jan. 1971, p. 23.

8—Bowlby, J. *Attachment and Loss,* Vol. 2: *Separation.* Basic Books. 1973, p. 190.

9—Ibid, pp. 115, 118.

10—Luce, Gay and Segal, Julius. *Insomnia.* Garden City, N.Y. Doubleday and Comp. 1969, p. 163.
11—Ibid, p. 159.

10. Siblings

1—Salk, Lee. *What Every Child Would Like His Parents To Know.* N.Y. McKay Comp. 1972, p. 14.

11. Marital Relations

1—Prescott, James W. "Cross-Cultural Studies." HEW, Growth and Development Branch, National Institute of Child Health and Human Development, Bethesda, Md. 20014.
2—Ibid.
3—Janov, A. *The Primal Scream.* N.Y. Simon and Schuster. 1973.
4—Ford, C. and Beach, F. *Patterns of Sexual Behavior.* N.Y. Harper and Row. 1951, p. 2.
5—Newton, Niles.
6—Ford, C. and Beach, F. *Patterns of Sexual Behavior.* N.Y. Harper and Row. 1951, p. 190.
7—Ibid, p. 189.
8—Ibid, p. 68.
9—Ibid, p. 2.
10—Gersh, M. *How to Raise Children at Home in your Spare Time.* Greenwich, Conn. Fawcett Publ. Inc. 1966.
11—Luce, Gay and Segal, J. *Insomnia.* Garden City, N.Y. Doubleday and Comp. 1969, p. 163.
12—Krebs. "Interruptus." *Psychology Today.* Jan. 1970, p. 153.
13—Cutler, Lucy. Minneapolis, Minn. 1973.
14—U.S. News and World Report, Oct. 1975, p. 32.

12. Special Circumstances

1—Hormann, Elizabeth. *Relactation: A Guide to Breastfeeding The Adopted Baby.* Mrs. Karl H. Hormann, 1 Merrill Ave., Belmont, Mass. 1971, p. 12.
2—Salk, Lee and Kramer, Rita. *How to Raise a Human Being.* N.Y. Random House. 1969, p. 13.

13. Nighttime Is for Sleeping!

1 —Luce, Gay and Segal, Julius. *Insomnia.* Garden City, N.Y. Doubleday and Comp. 1969, p. 162.

14. Conclusion

1 —Montagu, Ashley. *On Being Human.* N.Y. Hawthorn Books. 1966, p. 91.

2 —Benedict, Ruth. *Patterns of Culture.* Boston. Houghton, Mifflin. 1934.

3 —Bowlby, John. *Attachment and Loss,* Vol. 2: *Separation.* Basic Books. 1973.

4 —Montagu, Ashley. *On Being Human.* N.Y. Hawthorn Books. 1966, p. 111.

5 —Packard, Vance. *The Sexual Wilderness.* N.Y. McKay Comp. 1968, p. 33.

Bibliography

Books

Airola, Paavo, *Are You Confused,* Paavo Publ. P.O. Box 22001, Phoenix, Ariz. 1971.

Aldrich, C. Anderson, and Mary Aldrich, *Babies Are Human Beings.*

Aries, Philippe, *Centuries of Childhood,* N.Y. Alfred A. Knopf. 1962.

Baker, Carlos, *Ernest Hemingway,* N.Y. Scribner's Sons, 1969.

Bates, Marston and Abbott, Donald, *Coral Island,* N.Y. Scribner's Sons. 1958.

Benedict, Ruth, *Patterns of Culture,* Boston, Houghton-Mifflin. 1934.

Bible, Red Letter Edition, Book Inc. Publ. Boston, Mass.

Bowlby, John, *Attachment and Loss,* Vol. 2: *Separation,* Basic Books. 1973.

Brazelton, Berry, *Infants and Mothers,* N.Y. Dell Publ. Comp. Inc. 1969.

Cava, Esther Laden, *The Complete Question And Answer Book Of Child Training,* N.Y. Hawthorn Book Inc. 1972.

Chavasse, H., *Advice To A Wife,* N.Y. American News Comp. 1878.

Chisholm, Brock, *Prescription For Survival,* N.Y. Columbia Univ. Press. 1957.

Clymer, Swinburne, *The Mystery Of Sex And Race Regeneration,* Quakertown, Penn. Philosophical Publ. Comp. 1902.

Combe, A. *Management Of Infancy.* N.Y. Fowlers and Wells. 1840.

DeWees, W. *Treatise On The Physical And Medical Treatment Of Children,* Philadelphia, Carey, Lea and Carey. 1829.

Elkin, A.O. *The Australian Aborigines: How To Understand Them,* London, Angus and Robertson Ltd. 1945.

English, Spurgeon O. and Pearson, G. *Emotional Problems Of Living.*

Ericson, Eric, *Childhood And Society,* N.Y. W.W. Norton and Comp. 1963.

Ford, Clellan and Beach, Frank, *Patterns Of Sexual Behavior,* N.Y. Harper and Row, 1951.

Fraiberg, Selma, *The Magic Years,* N.Y. Scribner's Sons. 1959.

Fuller, John, *2,000,000,000 Guinea Pigs*, N.Y. Putnam. 1972.

Gathorne-Hardy, T., *The Unnatural History Of The Nanny*, Dial Press. New York, 1973.

Gerard, Alice, *Please Breastfeed Your Baby*, N.Y. New American Library. Pocket Book. 1970.

Gersch, Marvin, *How To Raise Children At Home In Your Spare Time*, Greenwich, Conn. Fawcett Publ., Inc. 1966.

Greenberg, J. *In This Sign*, Avon Books, 1972.

Haire, Doris, *The Cultural Warping Of Childbirth*, ICEA, Doris B. Haire, 251 Nottingham Way, Hillside, N.J. 1972.

Hass, Hans, *The Human Animal*, N.Y. Putnam's Sons. 1970.

Holt, Emmett, Jr. *Care And Feeding Of Children*, N.Y. Appleton-Century. 1943.

Homan, William, *Child Sense*, N.Y. Basic Books, Inc. 1969.

Hormann, Elizabeth, *Relactation: A Guide To Breastfeeding The Adopted Baby*, 1 Merril Ave., Belmont, Mass. 1971.

Hymes, James, *Child Under Six*, Englewood Cliffs, N.Y. Prentice Hall, Inc. 1963.

Janov, Arthur, *The Feeling Child*, N.Y. Simon and Schuster. 1973.

Janov, Arthur, *The Primal Scream*, N.Y. Dell Publ. 1970.

Josselyn, Irene, *Psychosocial Development Of Children*, Family Service Assoc. of America, N.Y. 1948.

Kippley, John and Sheila, *The Art Of Natural Family Planning*, P.O. Box 11084, Cincinnati, Ohio 45211.

Kippley, Sheila, *Breastfeeding And Natural Child Spacing*, N.Y. Harper and Row. 1974.

La Leche League International reprints, LLLI, 9616 Minneapolis Ave., Franklin Park, Ill. 60131.

La Leche League Manual, *The Womanly Art Of Breastfeeding*, LLLI, Franklin Park, Ill. 60131. 1958.

La Leche League of Minnesota Third State Seminar Transcripts, April, 1972, 9616 Minneapolis Avenue, Franklin Park, Ill. 60131.

La Leche League Third Biennial Convention Transcript LLLI, Franklin Park, Ill. 60131. 1968.

Langer, Lawrence, "The Pursuit of Happiness," an American Comedy. N.Y. Samuel French. 1934.

Lerich, Constance, *Maternity Nursing*. St. Louis, Mosby Co. 1970.

Lindgren, H. and Byrne, D. *Psychology*, N.Y. Wiley and Sons, Inc. 1971.

Lorenz, Konrad, *King Solomon's Ring*, N.Y. Crowell Comp. 1952.

Luce, Gay and Segal, Julius, *Insomnia*, Garden City, N.Y., Doubleday and Comp. 1969.

Luce, Gay and Segal, Julius, *Sleep*, N.Y. Coward-McGann, 1966.

Marlow, Dorothy, *Textbook Of Pediatric Nursing*, Philadelphia, Saunders Com. 1969.

Mead, Margaret, *From The South Seas*, N.Y. Morrow, 1939.

Moloney, James, *Fear: Contagion and Conquest*, Philosophical Library, N.Y. 1957.

Montagu, Ashley, *Man: His First Million Years*, N.Y. Mentor Book. 1957.

Montagu, Ashley, *The Natural Superiority Of Women*, N.Y., McMillan Comp. 1968.

Montagu, Ashley, *On Being Human*, N.Y. Hawthorn Book, Inc. 1966.

Montagu, Ashley, *Touching: The Human Significance of the Skin*, N.Y. Columbia Univ. Press. 1971.

Montessori, Maria, *The Absorbent Mind*, N.Y. Holt, Rinehart, and Winston, 1973.

Montessori, Maria, *The Secrets Of Childhood*, N.Y. Frederick Sotkes, 1939.

Morris, Desmond, *Intimate Behavior*, N.Y. Random House. 1971.

Neill, A.S., *Summerhill*, N.Y. Hart Publ. Comp. 1959.

Newton, Niles, *Family Book Of Child Care*, N.Y. Harper and Row. 1957.

Newton, Niles and Hoeber, Paul, *Maternal Emotions*, N.Y. Medical Book Depart. of Harper and Row, 1955.

Nichols, J.L., *Safe Counsel*, Chicago, Ill, Franklin Publ. 1928.

Packard, Vance, *The Sexual Wilderness*, N.Y. David McKay Comp. 1968.

Pryor, Karen, *Nursing Your Baby*. N.Y. Pocket Books, 1973.

Ribble, Margaret, *The Rights Of Infants*, N.Y. Columbia Univ. Press. 1965.

Richardson, S.A. et al, *Childbearing: Its Social And Psychological Aspects*, Williams and Wilkens. 1967.

Salk, Lee and Kramer, Rita, *How To Raise A Human Being*. N.Y. Random House. 1969.

Salk, Lee, *What Every Child Would Like His Parents To Know*. N.Y. McKay Comp. 1972.

Spock, Benjamin, *Baby And Child Care*. N.Y. Pocket Books. 1968.

Stiles, Henry Reed, *Bundling: Its Origin, Progress and Decline in America*, Albany, Knickerbocker Publ. 1871.

Thomas, Elizabeth, *The Harmless People*, N.Y., Knopf, 1959.

Ziegel, Erna and V. Blarcom, Carolyn, *Obstetric Nursing*, N.Y. McMillan Comp. 1972.

Magazines

Birth And Family Journal, Vol. 1, No. 3, 1974, Klaus, Marshall, editorial, 110 El Camino Real, Berkeley, Ca. 94705.

CEAN Today, Newsletter of CEA of Minneapolis and St. Paul, P.O. Box 20091, Minneapolis, Minn. 55420, Aug. 1973. "Ear Infections."

Child And Family Digest, Vol. 9, No. 3, P.O. Box 508, Oak Park, Ill. 1970.

Child And Family Quarterly, ed. Vol. 19, No. 4, 1960, Ed. Herbert Ratner, M.D., P.O. Box 508, Oak Park, Ill. p. 2.

Ethnology, Vol. 10, Barry, M. III, Paxson, L.M., "Infancy and Early Childhood: Cross-Cultural Codes 2," Oct. 1971.

Harvard Educational Review, Ryerson, Alice, "Medical Advice on Childrearing 1550-1900," Vol. 31, No. 3, p. 302.

House And Garden, Russel, "To Share or Not to Share," May, 1971. p. 98.

Marriage, Kenny and Schreiter, "Of Babies, Beds and Teddy Bears," Jan. 1971.

National Foundation Of Sudden Infant Death Pamphlet, "Facts About Sudden Infant Death Syndrome," 1501 Broadway, N.Y. 10036. 1970.

National Geographic, 1972. p. 244.

New Society, "Why Some Babies Don't Sleep," Bernal, Richard, Feb. 28, 1974, England.

Newsweek, "What Is a Mother to Do?" Sept. 23, 1968.

Obstetrical Society Of London, Martyh, W., "On the Management of Child-bed," 1870. p. 339.

Parents' Mag. Arnstein, Helene, "How Babies Learn to Wait," Dec. 1970.

Parents' Mag. Johnston, M. "Discipline or Indulgence?" July, 1969.

Parents' Mag. Whipple, Dorothy, "The Magic of Sleep," May, 1967.

Psychiatry, Montagu, Ashley, "Some Factors in Family Cohesion," Vol. 7, 1944.

Psychology Today, Breetveld, James, "Mother and Child in Africa," Feb. 1972. p. 63.

Psychology Today, Krebs, R., "Interruptus," Jan. 1970. p. 153.

Psychology Today, Newton, Niles, "Breastfeeding," Jn. 1968.

Reader's Digest, Ratcliff, J.D., "I'm Joe's Skin," June, 1972.

Redbook, Brecher, R., "Why Some Mothers Reject Their Babies," May 1966. p. 49.

Scientific American, Salk, Lee, "Role of the Heartbeat in the Relationship Between Mother and Infant," May 1973.

Scientific Digest Ed. Report on Sleep Research, June 1971. p. 57.

Scriber's Magazine, 1893.

Today's Health Mag., Cox, James, "When Bedtime Brings Problems," May, 1967.

U.S. Department Of Health, Education And Welfare, Washington, D.C., "Infant Care," 1967.

Appendix

THE SILVER BELL

A True Story of the Author's Own Experience

Listen! Above the dresser in my bedroom hangs a little bell. A silver bell. It's a family birthbell which, with joyful ringing, first announced the birth of my mother, then myself, and then rang for the birth of the first grandchild—my daughter, Yvonne.

One day I took it off the wall and, giving it a little shake, smiled at its clear, distinct sound. "Listen," it seemed to ring. "Remember to listen."

When Yvonne heard the sound she came into the room and asked, "What are you doing, Mama?" I shook the bell again and answered, "Listen. Remember to listen."

Somewhat puzzled, Yvonne looked at me. "Why?" she asked. For a moment I thought of all that had passed since her birth and then I answered, "Because listening will enrich your life. Listening is the first step in opening doors to friendship. It shows you care for others. And only by listening will you realize their care for you."

"But what has that got to do with the birthbell?" she asked. I placed my arm around her shoulder and said, "Come, I'll tell you."

It was twelve years ago when, full of confidence, I gently placed my newborn infant in her bassinet. I was proud and self-assured at the awesome responsibility of mothering. After all, I had read all the books and all I needed was a little cooperation and I would have the solution to any problem.

I shook that silver bell then. But little did I realize what painful, frightening, confusing sounds, what utter cacophony I would experience before I truly heard with clarity the meaning of that ring. "Listen. Remember to listen."

149

Oh, we had the usual moments of wavering, when things did not go as planned. Like any mother, I found some things perplexing. But, I figured, "She will learn."

One day, for instance, I decided it was time for her to eat her first spoonful of mashed banana. I placed her in her high chair and coaxed, "Open up. Here comes the airplane." But just as the airplane landed she stuck out her tongue. What a stubborn child, I thought. Why doesn't she listen to me? She should eat it.

When she was a year-and-a-half old, she began to protest at nap-time. She would stand up in her crib and cry. For a fleeting moment I thought perhaps I should lie down with her until she was asleep, and then carefully climb out. But I decided against it because I was afraid the crib would collapse.

So I put her in her bed, told her to go to sleep and walked away. As before she began to cry and this time she begged, "Mama, stay." But I did not really hear her plea. I only got frustrated because she did not cooperate with my scheme. I became angry at her crying because it made me feel powerless. So I ran away to the basement and waited, confused and very alone. And in the distance I heard her call me, "Mama."

At last it was quiet. I crept upstairs, and as I carefully approached the crib I saw my little baby child asleep. Yet even in her liberating sleep she was still sobbing. The words of Elizabeth Browning warned: "A child's sob in the silence curses deeper than a strong man in his wrath."

The daily agony continued, the battleground growing more fierce. With stubborn selfishness I listened only to myself, my own reasoning, and never once gave her a chance. I did not listen to her. I did not understand her. I did not know how. Instead I cried, "What is wrong with her?"

Then one evening while I was rocking her before bedtime, she began to weep, "Mama, stay." The crying intensified. Louder and louder she sobbed. She trembled. And I rocked and rocked. I rocked and rocked, rocked and rocked, back and forth, back and forth. And she cried and cried, and I rocked and rocked until at last I could not stand it any longer. I did not want to hear her anymore and I screamed, "Stop it."

In shocked silence the world stood still, and Yvonne lay her tear-drenched face upon my shoulder and whimpered.

Then it was as if God reached down and touched that silver bell. And as one who has lowered the hood of his cloak, I began to hear the meaning of that ring, "Listen. Remember to listen." And so, instead of putting her in her bed, I stayed.

Slowly I began to rock and softly, with a trembling voice, I began to hum a cradle song. When she was asleep I carefully put her down and looked into the face of a little angel. I whispered, "I'll begin to listen now."

Then a miracle happened. The brick wall of the tower, in which I had so securely placed myself, crumbled. As I began to listen I heard her fear, her needs, and her joys. One day she called, "Mama, look at the butterfly." I turned and looked and then we both ran down the street chasing butterflies. I felt closer to my children than I had ever felt before. I had discovered the joy of listening.

As I remembered to listen, I grew closer to my friends. By listening, I showed I really cared for them. By opening that door I began to know their friendship in return.

And so, my child, I shake this silver bell again, because my life has been enriched when I remember to listen.

And that, dear reader, is what this book has been all about; listening to the needs of your child and trusting in their innate goodness. Are things always going to go smoothly? No. Will it be rewarding? Yes. So open your mind and heart, with a special emphasis on co-family sleeping.

Index